WI
are saying about
Help! I'm in Charge

Help! I'm in Charge is an insightful look at working with and leading people. This isn't just another leadership book. Rod's unique take on challenges leaders face will make you laugh, think, and change. You're going to love this book!

—Rob Ketterling, lead pastor, River Valley Church, Savage, MN, and author of *Front-Row Leadership*

Help! I'm in Charge by Rod Loy is vintage Rod Loy . . . refreshingly honest, practical coaching for leaders who are human, who own it, and are bent on growing into the most effective leaders God has called them to be. Rod welcomes us into his own leadership journey and coaches us to keep learning with the inevitably unexpected aspects of leading real people. *Help! I'm in Charge* is direct, challenging, and humorous with hope—a welcome contribution from a leader-of-leaders we can enjoy following!

—Beth Grant, founder, Project Rescue, author of *Courageous Compassion*

I think every new leader has experienced that first moment of initial fear and wondered, *Now what?* Rod answers that question with practical principles that will help you become a God-honoring, difference-making leader!

—John McKinzie, lead pastor, Hope Fellowship, Frisco, TX

When I began leading, I dreamed of stimulating discussions over coffee with a wise leader. I searched for someone whom I respected to help me navigate my early experiences. *Help! I'm in Charge* is a response to that need. It's like a letter from a trusted friend, a wise soul, and a caring mentor to leaders of all ages. This book is full of valuable insights on leading with humility and navigating the pitfalls that surprise us along the way. It's been clear to me since the day I met Rod Loy that he's passionate about helping leaders, especially new leaders. Whether it's taking time to respond to questions on social media or inviting and hosting leaders at his church, he's generous with his time and resources. This is the kind of leader we should all long to emulate. I highly recommend this book!

—Lisa Russi, Project Rescue, France

Rod nails it! This book is practical help for anyone in a leadership position and a must-read for teams! Your team will benefit from learning and discussing principles that leaders rarely teach.

—David Wigington, lead pastor, Cornerstone Christian Fellowship, Bloomington, IN

When you do life with close friends you get to know them. Rod and I have been through many adventures together. We've travelled the dusty roads of Africa and ministered together in the church. Our goal has been to make a difference for Christ in the world. Over the years Rod has challenged me, through word and example, into a life that looks more like Jesus. Becoming more like Jesus means giving up "me" (my preferences, will, and actions) so I can reflect Christ. Rod strives for this reality in the way he leads the church and loves people. This book will encourage everyone who reads it and will help them become more like Christ.

—Scott Hanson, missionary

Biblical Christianity is often paradoxical: We live by dying. We find by losing. We advance by yielding. We lead by following. We keep by giving. With wit and wisdom Rod Loy writes that we must wane for Jesus to win. *Help! I'm in Charge* is for all those who long for Jesus to increase globally—and are willing to decrease daily for that to happen.

—Dick Brogden, missionary and author of *Live-Dead Joy*

HELP!
I'M IN CHARGE

Stuff Leadership Experts Didn't Tell You

Rod Loy

with Becca Winslow

First NLR
soul matters to God every

Books &
Resources
www.firstnlr.com

Dedication

This book is dedicated to the ministry of Project Rescue. When I began writing this book, my wife, Cindy, and I felt directed by God to donate all proceeds from this book to Project Rescue. We are delighted to partner with David and Beth Grant in this powerful ministry.

Project Rescue exists to rescue and restore victims of sexual slavery through the love and power of Jesus Christ. The mission is accomplished through holistic programs of physical, emotional, and spiritual intervention, prevention, and restoration for women and children in sexual slavery.

Project Rescue began in 1997 when K. K. Devaraj and team members from Bombay Teen Challenge went to Falkland Road in the red-light district of Mumbai, India, with a passion to reach a young generation ensnared by drugs, gangs, and prostitution. Their ministry team was stunned to find an estimated one hundred thousand women and children living in sexual slavery, many of whom had been sold by their impoverished families from North India and Nepal. In this first encounter, over one hundred women were challenged to new life in Jesus Christ. However, because they were in slavery they could not leave, but instead they asked K. K. Devaraj to take thirty-seven of their little daughters to a place of safety to prevent them from living a life of prostitution.

Out of that request Project Rescue and Bombay Teen Challenge created a safe aftercare home. The shelter became a secure environment where meals were shared, homework completed, and clean beds provided. Most importantly, the children were introduced to a Heavenly Father who loves them and has good purposes for them.

In the last twenty-one years, Project Rescue has grown far beyond that initial site. Last year Project Rescue ministered at sixteen sites in eight countries to more than forty thousand women and children impacted by sexual slavery. If you would like to know more about Project Rescue, donate, or learn how you can make a difference, please visit projectrescue.com

Contents

1

Are You Willing to Pay the Price?

One of the questions people often ask me is, "How can I succeed?" That's quickly followed by several other questions:

"Why do some people seem to get all the breaks?"

"Why can't I accomplish the things I want to?"

"Why do some people accomplish remarkable things, and other people don't?"

I generally answer those questions with two questions of my own. First, "Are you doing what you love and loving what you do?" When you meet someone who's a success, most of the time you'll discover they love what they do. A gifted pianist practices the piano five hours a day, because they love to play the piano. A pastor who is making a difference in the community loves working with people and leading the church. A skilled artist loves painting.

Here's a powerful principle: *You'll never fulfill your destiny doing something you despise.* When you love what you do, your chance to do it well is much greater. Not only will you do it well, but your passion will make you a contagious leader. When you love what you're doing, God will bring other people around you who will love working alongside you.

On the other hand, if you continually do things you dislike, there's a risk you'll eventually compromise your integrity. Why? If you don't like what you're doing, you'll be tempted to take short-cuts and take the easy way out.

Are there parts of my job I don't enjoy? Sure. There are moments in pastoring and leading people that bring frustration instead of satisfaction. There are parts of the job that make me tired and angry. But, for the most part, what I do makes my heart sing. I look forward to getting up in the morning and going to the church. I look forward to weekend services with great anticipation. I enjoy leading and working with a team. I love working with people as they progress through their spiritual journey.

The second key question I ask people is, "Are you willing to pay the price of success?" It may seem like some people get all the lucky breaks, but that isn't true. Over the years, I've learned a key to doing great things for God: *You must be willing to pay the price.*

Everything worth having costs you something.

This is the part of leadership and success people don't like to talk about. This isn't the fun part. We all enjoy the rewards. We look forward to the payoff. But this is the hard part: What's the cost associated with pursuing your vision? The question is not, "What do you want to do?" The question is, "What will it take for you to do it?" Any vision worth pursuing demands sacrifice and risk.

Doing great things for God will always take you outside your comfort zone. There are many unknowns associated with leadership and pursuing a vision. There are countless things that can go wrong. For a leader, risk and sacrifice are always associated with a vision. If God has birthed something in your heart, the day will come when you must sacrifice to achieve it. You'll have to make that sacrifice with no guarantee of success. If the cost and the risk cause you to become uncertain in your commitment, you'll fail. Furthermore, uncertainty in a leader is always magnified in the heart of a follower. If you aren't sure if the sacrifice is worth the vision, the people around you won't be willing to sacrifice for that vision.

We don't like to talk about paying a price. We like to talk about receiving rewards. It's much more popular to focus on what we'll get, what we'll accomplish, and what victory we'll experience. But the fact is, there will be a price to pay. If you want to make a difference, if you want to fulfill God's calling for your life, if you want to be a leader, you have to be willing to pay the price. This is the difference between changing the world and living your life without impact.

Some Basic Principles of Sacrifice

Everything worth having costs something.

There's a price to pay for everything you do. If you refuse to work, you'll go hungry. If you want to be the leader, you'll have to work more than other people. Nothing is free.

You might be thinking, *That's not true. Not everything has a cost. Salvation is free.* Not true. While salvation is free to you, it came at a high price! "You are not your own; you were bought at a price" (1 Corinthians 6:19–20).

The better the desired result, the higher the price.

My dream car is a Porsche Cayenne Turbo with 550 horsepower, 567-foot-pound of torque, and an 8-speed Tiptronic transmission. It's a wonderfully practical SUV that starts at $125,650.

You'd think for that price I would get all the options, but I recently went on the Porsche website and configured it exactly the way I want it and discovered that the price was just over $168,000! If you want the Porsche Cayenne Turbo with all the great options, that's what you must pay.

If you want to spend less money, you can buy a Smart Car. The Smart Car looks like one of those things you buy your three-year-old to pedal around the living room. It's not going to attract attention or win any races, but you can buy a Smart Car for just under $15,000.

If you aren't willing to pay the price, you must adjust your expectations.

There's no doubt the Porsche is a much better vehicle than the Smart Car. But the Porsche will cost you much, much more. In fact, you can buy eleven Smart Cars for the price of the Porsche Cayenne Turbo! The nicer the car— or the better the desired result—the higher the price.

The more you want to achieve, the higher the price you'll have to pay. The bigger your dreams and visions, the higher the price tag. Do you have big goals? If so, the price will be high. That's true no matter what you want.

- Olympians train for a lifetime.
- A surgeon spends over a decade in training.
- A concert violinist practices hundreds of hours every month for years.
- A pastor must live a life of integrity—under constant scrutiny—regardless of the circumstances.

The better the desired result, the higher the price. If you aren't willing to pay the price, you must adjust your expectations.

Those around you must understand the price and be willing to pay the price.

It isn't wise to assume others will automatically understand the price you're willing to pay. Those around you must understand clearly why the price is worth paying, and it's your job to help them understand that. You have to sell the results, the vision, and the dream.

When I hear a spouse complain about the time-commitment their spouse's dream requires, I know the spouse either doesn't understand the price or isn't willing to pay the price. If the people closest to you aren't willing for you to pay the price, you won't be able to pay it. I've watched many people fail to achieve their dreams simply because their spouse wasn't willing to pay the price.

I thank God for my wife, Cindy. I'm not willing to sacrifice my family for the ministry, but my family has always understood that there will be sacrifices in the ministry. We pay the price together. Cindy has never complained about what my ministry requires. Not once. Because she decided the price is worth paying, she's an invaluable partner and a powerful ally in achieving the dream. What we gain for the Kingdom is worth the price we pay together.

Never desire someone else's accomplishments until you first discover the price they paid.

Before you say you want to accomplish what someone else has accomplished, first determine the price they paid to achieve those accomplishments.

It's foolish to desire something without knowing the price. If you want a Porsche Cayenne Turbo, find out what it costs and decide if it's worth it to you. If you want what someone else has, it's likely you'll have to pay the price they have paid.

I've had people tell me, "Rod, you were just lucky. You had the right relationship with key mentors. Without that, you wouldn't have learned everything you've learned."

I wasn't lucky. At the age of sixteen I was attending Calvary Temple in Irving, Texas. I wanted my pastor, J. Don George, to be my mentor. Pastor George was leading an extremely large church. There was no reason for him to hang out with a sixteen-year-old kid! I knew that, so I looked for a way I could serve him so he would want to invest in me. When I discovered that he took all three of his family cars to the car wash every Saturday, I volunteered to do that for him. From the time I was sixteen until I was twenty-one, I took all three of his cars to the car wash—every Saturday. I never told him, "Sorry, I just can't make it today." Every week for six years, I took responsibility to see that his cars were clean.

It took several hours every Saturday. Often when I returned from the car wash with the last car, Pastor George would say, "Hey Rod, come in here and sit down." He would be doing the final edit on his sermon for the next morning and would talk about it with me. Other times, he took me to basketball games and football games. I spent hundreds of hours being mentored by a great leader, but I wasn't lucky! I paid a price for that relationship. I paid a price for the mentoring. It's foolish to desire someone else's accomplishments, unless you first discover the price they've paid.

High ambitions and low commitment equal foolish ambition.

In Luke, chapter 18, we find the story of the rich young ruler. As Jesus started on His way, a man ran up to Him, fell on his knees, and said:

> "Good teacher, what must I do to inherit eternal life?"
> "Why do you call me good?" Jesus answered. "No one is good—except God alone. You know the commandments: 'You shall not commit adultery, you shall not murder, you shall not steal, you shall not give false testimony, honor your father and mother.'"
> "All these I have kept since I was a boy," he said.
> When Jesus heard this, he said to him, "You still lack one thing. Sell everything you have and give to the poor, and you will have treasure in heaven. Then come, follow me."
> When he heard this, he became very sad, because he was very wealthy. (Luke 18:18-23)

That's one of the saddest stories in the Bible. The rich young ruler could have become a close follower of Jesus. He could have been an eyewitness to incredible miracles and become a leader in the Early Church . . . but none of that happened. He's included in the Bible only to serve as a negative example of someone who wasn't willing to pay the price.

The rich young ruler had lofty ambitions, but he wasn't willing to pay the price to achieve those ambitions. It's foolish to think you're smart or special enough to accomplish wonderful things without paying a great price. No one ever has. You won't either.

Your dream may be exciting, but if you aren't willing to pay the accompanying price, it's not a dream . . . it's a fantasy. If you want to have a great marriage, there's a price to pay. Are you willing to pay the price? If you want to be a doctor or play in the NBA, there's a price to pay. If you want to be a missionary whose ministry changes the world, there's a price to pay. The higher your goal and the greater the commitment required, the more intensely you must be committed to pay the price.

You can detect a person's destiny by the price they're willing to pay.

We once had a staff member who complained about how hard our team worked. That let me know he wasn't destined for greatness unless he changed his willingness to pay the price. You can spot this early in life. Thousands of little boys say, "I want to play in the NBA." But only a few of them practice six hours a day. Those are the ones who have a chance to fulfill their dream. You can detect their destiny by the price they're willing to pay.

Recently, I spoke at a large conference. At the end of my first session, I had a line of people ask me to mentor them. So, at the start of my second session, I said, "I won't mentor anyone unless they first commit to read twenty-four books a year. Because if you won't read (or listen to) at least two books a month, you're not willing to pay a high enough price for me to invest in you." At the end of that session the line had vanished. No one was willing to pay the price. You can detect someone's future by the price they're willing to pay.

The Bible uses a flattering term for people who aren't willing to pay the price for their dreams: They're called "sluggards." I know that sounds harsh, but it's not my word! Not only does Proverbs describe these individuals as so lazy that they turn on their beds "as a door turns on its hinges" (26:14), but it also points out that because of their unwillingness to work, the sluggard's dream actually becomes their downfall: "The craving of the sluggard will be the death of him, because his hands refuse to work" (21:25). On the other hand, those who are willing to pay the price will reap the rewards: "A sluggard's appetite is never filled, but the desires of the diligent are fully satisfied" (13:4). Do you want your dream "fully satisfied"? Be diligent. Pay the price—and keep paying the price.

> **Your dream may be exciting, but if you aren't willing to pay the accompanying price, it's not a dream . . . it's a fantasy.**

If you complain about the price, you won't pay it for long.

Not only must you be willing to pay the price, you must be willing to continue paying the price. When I hear someone complain about how hard they work, I think, *Most likely they'll never accomplish wonderful things.*

I recently watched an episode of *Shark Tank*. One of the sharks, Robert Herjavec, told an entrepreneur that he only slept four hours a night because he would rather be rich than rested. While I may not think his goal is admirable, his commitment to it certainly is!

At our church we have a group of volunteers who make an eight-year commitment to be class pastors. They lead and pastor one class from sixth grade until their first year of college! Being a class pastor is the longest and most difficult commitment anyone at our church makes. It's spiritually, emotionally, and physically demanding, but you never hear our class pastors complain. They knew hard work was part of the deal when they agreed to be a pastor, and their desire to see young people grow into mature, life-long followers of Jesus makes all the work worth it. That's the price they're willing to pay.

Everyone who has accomplished great things for God has paid an extraordinary price.

Paul wrote much of the New Testament and was the key missionary who launched the Early Church. Under his leadership, the gospel spread across the known world. Paul did amazing things for the kingdom of God, but he paid a high price.

> Five times I received from the Jews the forty lashes minus one. Three times I was beaten with rods, once I was pelted with stones, three times I was ship-wrecked, I spent a night and a day in the open sea, I have been constantly on the move. I have been in danger from rivers, in danger from bandits, in danger from my fellow Jews, in danger from Gentiles; in danger in the city, in danger in the country, in danger at sea; and in danger from false believers. I have labored and toiled and have often gone without sleep; I have known hunger and thirst and have often gone without

food; I have been cold and naked. Besides everything else, I face daily the pressure of my concern for all the churches. (2 Corinthians 11:24-28)

Esther was an orphan during the Persian Empire who—contrary to the Hollywood version of her story—was crowned queen after being forcibly taken from her home as a young woman and trafficked to the king as a concubine. In the middle of this hardship, God asked her to take a stand for her people, the Jews, because the king's decree threatened to annihilate them. Esther would have to confess that she, herself, was a Jew and approach the king, unbidden—an offense punishable by death. Talk about a high price! But Esther looked beyond herself to the hardship of her people and took the risk, not only saving herself but her people.

Moses gave up everything he knew and did things that stretched him entirely out of his comfort zone to obey God and lead the Jewish people out of slavery.

Mary—young and unwed—gave up her good name and reputation to become God's instrument to bring His Son into the world.

Many years ago, a South African missionary couple went to work among the Somali people of northern Kenya. They went to a town named Garissa where they lived and worked among the people. After living there several years, their baby son, Hendrick, was born.

Gradually, Hendrick developed a mysterious illness. He became sicker and sicker, and finally died at the age of two. Through a series of events the parents discovered Hendrick had slowly been poisoned to death by people in the Somali community who were opposed to the church and wanted the missionaries to leave. Their son was killed by the people to whom they ministered. At Hendrick's funeral, his father said to the Muslim leaders in the community, "You think we're going away, but we're not. Every time you walk by this grave, it will remind you there was a father who loved you enough to let his son die here so you can know the love of Jesus."

A couple of years ago I stood at that grave. Tears poured down my face as I thought about the sacrifice that family made to share Jesus. They paid an incredibly high price. As I wept and prayed, I was challenged and convicted by the question: "What is Jesus worth to *me*? What price am *I* willing to pay?"

Rachel is twenty years old. Last summer she spent two months in an incredibly dangerous place, living among an unreached people group who are known as terrorists who hate Americans. Rachel lived in a slum, walked through dangerous streets every day, and shared Jesus with people who had never heard about His love.

I interviewed Rachel in our Wednesday night service for students. I asked her, "Why? Why would you go to a difficult, dangerous place where people hate you?"

Her reply was powerful. "What's the worst thing that could happen to me? They could kill me? If they did that, I'd be in heaven with Jesus for all eternity. But if they die, they won't have that privilege—unless someone is willing to go and tell them."

The room was silent. Then Rachel added, "Jesus is worth it."

Rachel is willing to pay a high price. Now you may think she's just young and reckless, or you may think that as her spiritual leader I have a responsibility to discourage such an extreme perspective. What you don't see, and what Rachel understands, is that her willingness is merely a refusal to limit God by shrinking back from the high price of obedience.

Everyone who has accomplished great things for God has paid an extraordinary price. You won't accomplish great things without paying a great price.

The people who work with you will never pay a higher price than you.

Don't expect the people in your organization to be radically committed when you're not. Don't expect your kids' commitment to be any higher than yours. Don't expect your family or your followers to pay a price you're not willing to pay.

I work the most hours in our organization. Why? Because the leader pays the highest price. Your children, your coworkers, and your followers are watching to see what price you pay. If you want to lead, you must be willing to pay the price—and pay it first.

When we needed to open more parking at our church, I moved my parking spot. I put up a "Reserved for Pastor" sign at the farthest spot in the most remote lot. I paid guys to come paint over the reserved spaces close to the building, and the other pastors joined me in parking half a mile away. We did that because we knew we had to pay the price if we were going to ask others to pay it. If you want to lead, there's a price to pay. Leaders who pay the price produce followers who pay the price.

You'll be rewarded according to the price you're willing to pay, not just according to your ability.

Think of the famous Bible story of David and Goliath. Could other people have killed the giant Goliath? There were probably better marksmen who were more skilled at the slingshot than the shepherd boy David. Someone else probably could have killed Goliath, but no one else did. Why? Because they weren't willing to take the risk. David was willing to pay a price no one else was willing to pay.

Do you want to get promoted on your job? Do you want to receive a raise? Do you want to accomplish great things? Pay the highest price!

I started working at my church when I was eighteen years old. One of the first things I did was figure out what time the pastor arrived at the church. As soon as I learned it, I made sure to get there at least five minutes before him every day—including Sunday. For all he knew, I got there two hours before him! I didn't care. I just wanted to be there first. I wanted him to see my willingness to pay the price. I was surrounded by far more talented people, but no one was more willing to pay the price. My reward was great! I earned the trust and respect of my leader. It was well worth the price.

> **There are lots of talented people who never accomplish anything because they're simply not willing to pay the price.**

The price you pay is more important than the talent you possess.

Ability isn't enough. There are lots of talented people who never accomplish anything because they're simply not willing to pay the price. I could introduce you to a lot of talented failures.

In ministry, I can introduce you to incredibly talented people who are doing very little for God. They simply aren't willing to pay the price required for success—whether that's time, effort, or simply getting out of bed.

Years ago, I sat at a restaurant with a friend of mine. He was the most phenomenally talented guy I've ever met. He could do anything . . . absolutely anything. He was smart, witty, funny, talented, and charismatic. He had it all. I looked at him and said, "You've got more talent in your little finger than I have in my whole body, but you'll never achieve what I'll achieve because you're not willing to pay the price." Sadly, I was right. His life has demonstrated that. Twenty years later, he still has extraordinary talent, and he's still not willing to pay a high price. He's an incredibly talented failure. Talent may open the door but paying the price will keep you there.

Those who are willing to pay a high price will always be criticized by those who are not.

Why? Because it makes the critics feel insecure. Your willingness exposes their unwillingness, so they look for things to criticize. The higher the price you pay, the more opposition you can expect. People don't want you to be an extraordinary world-changer. They want to limit your vision and limit your dream. They want you to be just like them: average. They don't want you to achieve great things because they haven't achieved them. Pay the price anyway. Dare to be more than average!

Take a hard look at the negative, critical people you know. Have you got one in mind? Good. Let me ask you a couple of questions about them.

What have they done for God?

What have they accomplished?

What degree of success have they achieved?

I've never met a negative person who's made a significant impact for good. Your critics are exactly that—critics. Instead of making a difference, they look for ways to talk you out of making a difference. Why would you let foolish critics discourage you from making a difference? Do great things for God—in spite of the critics!

Always determine the price you are willing to pay.

Would you go to a car dealer, pick out car, and say, "I'll just pay whatever you want me to pay. You pick it. I don't even need to see the price." You would never do that. If you're smart, you go to the showroom with a maximum price in mind. Then all you have to do is determine if the dream car is worth the price. If it's not, then you adjust your car selection to match the price you're willing to pay.

Years ago, Cindy and I went to the Olympic training center in Colorado Springs. It's an amazing place. We weren't on a tour; instead, we just walked around the facility with a couple of friends. (Wow, security sure is different now!) We stood at a window and looked in the gym where the women's gymnastics team was practicing. One of the coaches came to the door, opened it, and said, "You can come in if you promise not to make any noise. You can't talk or ask questions. You can just sit there and watch."

We sat just off the edge of the mat and watched one gymnast work on her floor routine. She was working on one position:

the angle of her foot when she landed at the end of a run. For one hour that was all she did. Over and over and over again she worked on the angle of that foot. I'm not a gymnastics enthusiast, but I was amazed.

When we were done we walked out of the Olympic training center and there in front of us was a countdown clock to the next Olympics. It showed 1,008 days. That gymnast's event was 1,008 days away, and she was working all day on the angle of her foot. I was awestruck at the extraordinary price she was willing to pay to achieve her dream.

Over two-and-a-half years later, Cindy and I watched on TV as that gymnast won an Olympic medal. Her routine looked effortless and natural—and the angle of her foot on the landing was perfect!

Always determine the price you're willing to pay. What is it worth to you to be the best? What price are you willing to pay to take the gospel to people who have never heard or to build a business that makes a difference? Decide in advance what sacrifices you are willing to make.

Bless those who pay the price with you and keep them in your life.

Along the way God will send people who will willingly join you in paying the price. Bless them, don't ever forget them, and do everything you can to keep them in your life.

As a young leader, I foolishly thought there would be an unending supply of these people, that there would always be others willing to pay the price with me. I've learned differently. There have been those I thought would pay the price, but it didn't turn

out that way. There were others I should have kept in close relationship. Bless those who pay the price with you and do whatever
it takes to keep them in your life.

**Don't disdain or be frustrated with the rare leader who
candidly communicates the price.**

Jesus was an amazing leader. When He gave the marching orders
to His disciples, He communicated the price in a powerful way:

> "Then you will be handed over to be persecuted and put
> to death, and you will be hated by all nations because
> of me. At that time many will turn away from the
> faith and will betray and hate each other, and many
> false prophets will appear and deceive many people.
> Because of the increase of wickedness, the love of most
> will grow cold, but the one who stands firm to the end
> will be saved." (Matthew 24:9–13)

Understand, these were the guys Jesus recruited to start the
church. This was their pep talk! Jesus clearly identified the price
for them.

You can almost imagine the disciples saying, "Whoa! Hold on!
Persecuted and put to death? You haven't really mentioned that
before!" Jesus communicated the price, but then He let His followers know what would happen because they were willing to pay it:

> "And this gospel of the kingdom will be preached in the
> whole world as a testimony to all nations, and then the
> end will come." (Matthew 24:14)

There are rare leaders who candidly communicate the price. They know what it takes, and they communicate the price others will have to pay. Ultimately, that kind of leader attracts incredible followers. They may not have the biggest group, but they have an incredibly committed team!

Do you want to follow a great leader? Follow one who doesn't sell you on false optimism but instead says, "This will be the hardest thing you'll ever do in your life. You'll be criticized. People are going to turn their backs on you. You're going to be hurt. Your feelings will be hurt. This will be hard. It's going to take a huge amount of time, energy, and effort. But when you finish, you'll have changed the world. You'll have made a difference for eternity."

The greatest leader in the history of the world was Jesus. He selected a handful of misfits who didn't have any track record of speaking or leading: tax collectors, fishermen, and common people. Those were the people Jesus chose to mentor, and the people who changed the world. We still read their stories today!

The most incredible leader of all time, Jesus paid the ultimate price. The price wasn't a surprise to Him. He determined ahead of time the price was worth it. He determined you were worth saving, that your salvation was worth His life.

If you want to do amazing things for God, if you want to make a difference, if you want your life to count, if you want to reach your friends for Jesus, you'll have to pay a price. You can do it with God's help. The question is: Will you? Your willingness to pay the price will determine the answer. The price you pay will determine the greatness you achieve.

Stuff to consider . . .

1. What is your dream? What will it cost you? What price are you not willing to pay? Why/why not?

2. Is there a dream in your heart that hasn't caught traction? Chances are, you haven't identified a price you would pay to move toward that dream. Make a list of the personal sacrifices you could make, information you could learn, skills you could refine, gaps you could fill in the life of a mentor around you in exchange for access—anything and everything you could do right now to move forward.

3. If you're a team leader, consider whether you've adequately sold your vision and dream to your team. What could you do to reestablish the dream?

2

The One Thing You Can Expect
Is the Unexpected

As I drove back to my office from a meeting I received the news that one of the pillars of our church, Carroll Murry, had passed away. Carroll was a lifelong member, a faithful supporter, and a dear friend.

Cindy and I were scheduled to leave town the next day. We planned to speak at a meeting, then spend an extra day or two in rest and relaxation. I'm not always able to cancel trips when I'm scheduled to speak, but for this trip, I called Cindy, let her know what had happened, and we started changing our plans. We cancelled plane tickets, hotel reservations, and other plans. Cindy was sad . . . for about thirty seconds. Then, she moved on. I called one of our other pastors to let him know I was going to be in town. He said, "I don't know how you do it. How do you deal with unexpected changes so easily?"

That night, at our young adult service, I listened to Pastor Dave and Cheryl Richards share the story of their journey. They talked about a failed marriage in Dave's past, divorce, abandonment, and a bout with cancer. By the time they were done speaking, my cancelled trip and time away didn't seem like a sacrifice at all.

I've learned that unexpected change is just part of life as a leader. Things happen. About the only thing you can expect is that the unexpected will happen.

A few years ago, I had scheduled a week alone with God the first of May. I needed to study, pray, and spend time in reflection, so we rented a beautiful cabin in a quiet place. I was planning to leave on Sunday afternoon, but Saturday night brought a crisis. A key couple in our church were in the middle of a devastating marriage issue.

I couldn't leave. I had to stay. I was deeply disappointed . . . for about thirty minutes. Then my focus shifted to what was in front of me. One of our staff asked me, "How do you keep from going crazy? How do you handle it? How do you deal with sudden changes to your schedule or your priorities and not lose it?"

Whether it's schedule, family, ministry, or a vacation, how do you deal with a crisis, a change of plans, or a challenge? You have your week, year, marriage, or life all laid out and suddenly something takes it another direction. The doctor calls with shocking news. You lose your job at a key time for your family. Your company mandates a transfer. A best friend passes away. Someone you thought was your friend turns out to be anything but. These things happen. It's inevitable. In fact, Jesus cautioned us, "In this world you will have trouble" (John 16:33).

Your carefully thought-out plans can be blown out of the water in a moment. That's all part of living in this world. When it happens, what do you do? How do you keep it together? How do you handle the unexpected moments of life? Before I give you a list of ways to manage life's crises, I want to tell you how important your response is in those moments. In life's unexpected challenges and crises, your response reveals many things to the people watching you.

What Your Response Reveals about You

Your response to the unexpected reveals your level of trust in God.

It's easy to trust God when everything is going well and as expected. In fact, that doesn't take much trust at all. Why would you need to trust if everything is predictable, stable, and planned? But when things go differently than you had planned, whether it's a missed flight or a bad doctor's report, your response to that situation reveals your level of trust in God—to yourself and to others.

I used to get really upset if I missed a flight or had an unexpected travel delay. Finally, I realized, *If I can't trust the Lord with a missed flight, how will I ever trust Him with life's bigger challenges?*

Solomon wrote, "Trust in the LORD with all your heart and lean not on your own understanding; in all your ways submit to him, and he will make your paths straight" (Proverbs 3:5–6). I think a key word in that admonition is "all." Trust in the Lord with *all* your heart. Trust the Lord in *all* your ways, both big and small. The people who are watching how you respond to the unexpected events in life will learn what trust looks like and be encouraged to practice it!

Your response to the unexpected reveals your level of confidence in your purpose and call.

When you know your purpose in life and what you're called to do, you weather unexpected storms differently from people who have no goals or purpose. You're less likely to get stuck in a difficult moment when you're motivated by your purpose. Knowing God's greater plan for you keeps you moving forward.

Peter described it this way: "Therefore, my brothers and sisters, make every effort to confirm your calling and election. For if you do these things, you will never stumble" (2 Peter 1:10).

Your response to the unexpected reveals your ability to help others when they encounter a storm.

People watch for your response when you face the unexpected. If you don't deal well with your situation, people lose confidence in your ability to help them in their crisis. After all, if you can't keep it together during your challenges, how can you teach them? Getting help from someone who panics is kind of like going to a bankrupt financial planner or a homeless homebuilder. It doesn't make sense.

> **Knowing God's greater plan for you keeps you moving forward.**

Wise leaders recognize that God will use their difficulties to help others face life's difficulties. Last year my wife, Cindy, was diagnosed with kidney cancer. My tendency was to stay quiet and not share this information with others, but Cindy was determined to live out her cancer journey openly, in front of friends, our congregation, and even the Facebook world. She knew that her confident reaction to cancer could serve as an encouragement to others who faced the same diagnosis.

Paul's words of encouragement can help us through the challenging times:

> **What a wonderful God we have—he is the Father of our Lord Jesus Christ, the source of every mercy, and the one who so wonderfully comforts and strengthens us**

in our hardships and trials. And why does he do this? So that when others are troubled, needing our sympathy and encouragement, we can pass on to them this same help and comfort God has given us. You can be sure that the more we undergo sufferings for Christ, the more he will shower us with his comfort and encouragement. (2 Corinthians 1:3–5, TLB)

Your response to the unexpected reveals your maturity.

How do immature people react when they don't get their way? They get mad, throw a fit, and lose control—and that's not just preschoolers! In fact, that kind of behavior has nothing to do with age! I've known remarkably mature young leaders and desperately immature older leaders. I've watched people who should know better throw a fit when their classroom is not set up the way they expected, or when they must change parking places. They may be old, but they sure aren't mature!

Any leader can handle the expected. Any leader can lead in the good times, when everything is going well, but remember this: "You are a poor specimen if you can't stand the pressure of adversity" (Proverbs 24:10, TLB). Moments of crisis reveal great leaders. Their response is a beacon of hope to everyone who is watching them. Every unexpected crisis will reveal what's inside you—both to yourself and to others.

How to Handle the Unexpected

If you want to lead well in a crisis, you must decide in advance how you'll face the unexpected moments when they happen. Here are some thoughts and principles to help you.

Don't freak out.

First, freaking out doesn't help. It doesn't solve the problem. In fact, it often makes the problem worse! Furthermore, when you're done freaking out, there's still a challenge to face. All you did was lose time.

Second, when you freak out it creates uncertainty in everyone around you. They no longer have a leader they can trust and follow. When you freak out, you're no longer the leader; you're just another freaked-out follower.

How do you keep from freaking out? Expect the unexpected. If you expect challenges and crises, you won't be surprised and freaked out when they happen. "Dear friends, do not be surprised [in other words, don't freak out] at the fiery ordeal that has come on you to test you, as though something strange were happening to you. But rejoice inasmuch as you participate in the sufferings of Christ, so that you may be overjoyed when his glory is revealed" (1 Peter 4:12–13).

Hardships and trials are a normal part of life; they're par for the course. When you anticipate them, you position yourself to rejoice rather than to lose your cool when they happen.

Don't make the situation global.

When a crisis comes, some people say things like:

"Everything bad happens to me."
"Things always go wrong in my life."
"Why me? How can one person deal with so much?"
"Why do these things always happen to me?"
"How can I take one more thing?"

Resist the temptation to bunch crises together in your mind. Instead, deal with today's challenge in isolation from what has happened before and what may happen in the future. Approach the crisis by saying, "This thing in front of me right now has absolutely nothing to do with anything else that has happened to me. This is just another challenge I get to face." That isn't easy, but it'll keep you from combining a few manageable things into an overwhelming thing!

If bunching crises consistently gets you in a rut, fight the temptation to do that by bunching blessings together instead. David is an incredible biblical example of a leader who refused to let a current crisis determine his outlook. At Ziklag, amidst unthinkable personal hardship (his family and those of all his men had been captured by the enemy and his men were discussing whether to stone him), he "found strength in the LORD his God" (1 Samuel 30:6). The Psalms are filled with evidence of David's determination to "praise the LORD . . . and forget not all his benefits" (Psalm 103:2).

Moments of crisis reveal great leaders.

Keep things in perspective.

Paul wrote: "I consider that our present sufferings are not worth comparing with the glory that will be revealed in us" (Romans 8:18.) Ask yourself, "In light of eternity, in light of the long run, how do I view this unexpected situation?" When Paul talked about his experiences of imprisonment, beatings, stoning, persecution, and shipwrecks he described them as momentary afflictions because he had his mind fixed on his goal: eternity with Jesus Christ. Paul said, "All those things aren't worthy to be compared to the glory that is waiting for me."

When the doctors diagnosed Cindy's cancer, instead of saying, "Why me?" she said, "Why not me? Is there anything special about me that says I shouldn't get sick?" Initially, we didn't know the prognosis, but we knew God's ultimate plan for our lives. No one has promised us a trouble-free life in this world—but we know heaven is ahead of us! That perspective keeps us from overreacting to the inevitable problems in this world.

Resist negative emotions.

There are natural, predictable responses to the unexpected. It's natural to respond to an unexpected crisis with dejection, depression, or even despair. But godly leaders fight that pattern of thinking with the truth of God's Word and by stepping back to look at the big picture.

> **No one has promised us a trouble-free life in this world—but we know heaven is ahead of us!**

Let me encourage you to fight initial negative responses by filling your mind with the positive truths of Scripture. "Don't copy the behavior and customs of this world, but let God transform you into a new person by changing the way you think. Then you will learn to know God's will for you, which is good and pleasing and perfect" (Romans 12:2, NLT). You can also fight negative emotions with healthy nutrition, rest, and exercise. If you surround yourself with positive people, they'll help you replace negative feelings with positive feelings. Above all, keep your focus on Christ rather than on the circumstance.

Remember, this is part of the deal.

I often remind myself, "When I signed up for ministry, unexpected challenges were part of the deal. I knew all along there would be difficulties, crises, and moments that interrupted my schedule and agenda."

You might not be in ministry, but you can think the same way. *When I decided to have children, challenges came with it. I knew the kids would get sick, get in trouble, and misbehave. That's part of being a parent. I signed up for this!*

At your wedding, you may have repeated a vow, "for better or for worse." When you said that, you were probably thinking about better, not worse! But worse comes. Sickness, arguments, disagreements, and disappointment are all part of the deal. You signed up for this!

On the day you decided to buy a car, you knew that one day that beautiful, shiny piece of machinery would break down. One day it wouldn't start. You'd have flat tires, get door dings, and need new parts. That's part of buying a car. You signed up for that!

Hard times and unexpected difficulties are part of life's deal. Everyone faces them, even followers of Jesus. Paul warned his young follower Timothy that challenging times would come: "But you should keep a clear mind in every situation. Don't be afraid of suffering for the Lord. Work at telling others the Good News, and fully carry out the ministry God has given you" (2 Timothy 4:5, NLT).

Leaders aren't immune from trouble. It's part of the deal. Remember what Jesus promised, "Here on earth you will have many trials and sorrows. But take heart, because I have overcome the world" (John 16:33, NLT).

Don't play the "if only" game.

The "if only" game will put you in a depressed mood faster than anything else.

If only I had been a better example.

If only I had left home five minutes later, I wouldn't have had the accident.

If only I had been there to help.

If only I had finished college.

If only I had better leadership skills.

"If only" is evaluating the past from a negative perspective. It's never productive and often limits your capacity to fulfill God's call on your life for that assignment. The apostle Paul certainly had reasons to play the "if only" game. Not many church leaders persecuted and killed Christians in their previous jobs. Yet when Paul discussed his past as a devout Jew and callous persecutor, he didn't wallow in guilt and say "if only." Instead, he boldly declared, "Forgetting what is behind and straining toward what is ahead, I press on toward the goal to win the prize for which God has called me heavenward in Christ Jesus" (Philippians 3:13–14). Like Paul, let the past remain in the past . . . and move forward.

Avoid enablers.

When you face a difficulty there's a tendency to gravitate toward people who will feel sorry for you and commiserate with you. It's tempting to share how bad you have it to gain their sympathy, but that works against you in the long run. It reinforces a negative outlook in your mind, rather than a positive outlook.

Enablers don't get you out of the cycle of feeling down; they keep you there! In many instances, they find their sense of worth when a person who feels bad confides in them, which means they aren't focused on helping that person rise above the problems and pain. They enjoy feeling needed.

It's much more productive to surround yourself with positive people who are focused on life's greater purpose and will refuse to let you wallow in self-pity. Get around people who will tell you, "Get off your couch. This isn't the end of life. Quit acting that way and let's go!"

> **Leaders aren't immune from trouble. It's part of the deal.**

Wait a second! I thought you said "positive people"? People who firmly and lovingly help you frame a crisis in truth are positive people. Positive people approach the unexpected not by acting as if it didn't happen, but by looking it squarely in the face and saying, "It's here. Now let's deal with it."

Find a safe place to talk.

Find one person who can be a safe confidant and will challenge you if you're projecting, blaming, or just thinking the wrong things, because whenever you're in the middle of crisis it's likely that you are projecting, blaming, or thinking the wrong things to some degree. Talk the situation through with someone honest enough to tell you to shut up and get over it. That's one reason you need a church family. Church is a wonderful place to find safe, positive, encouraging people who will help you walk out of the valley of despair.

Keep going.

Never allow an event or series of events to make you doubt your mission and purpose. The Bible tells us that "our struggle is not against flesh and blood, but against the rulers, against the authorities, against the powers of this dark world and against the spiritual forces of evil in the heavenly realms" (Ephesians 6:12). We face a real enemy who is happy to get us offtrack if he can. I've seen people resist the call of God on their lives when they faced opposition. Just because bad things happen doesn't necessarily mean you're out of the will of God. Keep going until He shuts the door or opens a new one.

Whatever you do, don't shut down! Paul said, "That is why we never give up. Though our bodies are dying, our spirits are being renewed every day. For our present troubles are small and won't last very long. Yet they produce for us a glory that vastly outweighs them and will last forever" (2 Corinthians 4:16–17, NLT). This crisis or challenge won't last forever, but will produce in you a strength and trust to carry you through the next crisis!

Do one thing at a time.

In the middle of the unexpected, it can seem that life is spiraling out of control. To regain some semblance of order, people have the tendency to multitask. The longer and more complex their task list, the more they feel in control. Not only does this distraction offer a false sense of control, it also gets overwhelming pretty quickly. You'll end up doing a bunch of insignificant things poorly rather than doing the important things well.

Often the unexpected is dealing with someone else's crisis. In those instances, do what you can. Help where you can. Release what you can't. People ask me, "How do you sleep at night with all the things you deal with?" I do what I can. I can't do what I can't do. That's God's job. I can't do His job.

Do what you can: Look for a job. Get a second opinion. Read a book. Get advice from wise counsel. Do what you can . . . then release what you can't to "him who is able to do immeasurably more than all we ask or imagine, according to his power that is at work within us" (Ephesians 3:20).

Don't project disappointment and anger.

When you project disappointment and anger, it usually shows up as blame and criticism. I see this all the time. When something goes wrong, people look for someone to blame. Rather than deal with the situation, they blame someone or something for it. When they do that, they're projecting. When life isn't going as someone expected, they project their disappointment and anger onto others.

I can tell when a marriage is struggling. A husband and wife who were both positive people suddenly become negative, complaining cynics. They're projecting their marital storm into other areas of their lives.

When people lose their jobs, they often become controlling and critical at church and at home. They're simply projecting their disappointment and anger onto others.

There's a better way to handle the unsettling emotions of an unexpected crisis: Get in God's presence. Spend time in prayer and worship—and don't stop until you're changed, until you feel peace. This should have been first on the list because this is the very first thing I do to handle unexpected situations. When the unexpected steals your peace and you feel anxious and worried, deal with that by returning to the Source of peace.

The apostle Paul said it this way:

> Don't worry about anything; instead, pray about everything. Tell God what you need, and thank him for all he has done. Then you will experience God's peace, which exceeds anything we can understand. His peace will guard your hearts and minds as you live in Christ Jesus. (Philippians 4:6-7, NLT)

Do what is right, regardless of how you feel. There's a right thing to do. Do that. Do right in that moment and then in the next moment. Be faithful to God, His Word, and His commands. God rewards and blesses the faithful!

Stuff to consider . . .

1. Think of a recent unexpected event that happened to you. How did you respond to that situation? Consider how you might respond better in the future.

2. How does our response to a crisis reveal our trust in God?

3. List some ways your response to the unexpected affects those watching you as a leader.

4. God's Word can help us keep our emotions in check during a crisis. List some verses that have helped you weather a crisis.

3

We All Make Monumental Mistakes

I will be the first to admit that I've made some monumental mistakes in my life. When you speak in public as much as I do, mistakes are inevitable. I've called people by their wrong names. I've messed up and thought I was in a different city. When you're speaking in Fort Meyers and you tell the crowd, "It's good to be in Sarasota," that doesn't go over very well. I've said things and later thought, *What in the world did that mean?* or *Why did I say that? I don't even agree with that!*

A couple months ago, at the start of my message, I wanted to direct our congregation to an insert in their bulletin, but I said, "I put an *insult* in your bulletin today." When everyone started laughing, I knew I couldn't go on without acknowledging my mistake.

Another time, while speaking, I forgot the name of the host pastor. I frantically looked at my notes, hoping I had written it down. No luck. Finally, rather than just saying, "I appreciate your pastor very much," I decided to risk that his name was "John." When I said, "Thank you, Pastor John, for inviting me here," the room grew still. From behind me, the pastor whispered loudly, "That was the last pastor. My name is Greg." There was no way out of that one!

Public speakers aren't the only ones who make mistakes. We all make them. In fact, mistakes are big business. We call them bloopers. Entire TV shows are based on people's mistakes. Aren't you glad all your mistakes aren't captured on camera and played for the world to see? I'm certainly glad no one has made a film of my mistakes, though I've made enough of them to qualify for a lifetime achievement award.

If you want more responsibility, you must be willing to accept visibility and accountability.

Now you're probably wondering, *So what do mistakes have to do with leadership?* Think about it. If the president makes a mistake, it appears on the front page of newspapers around the world. The guy who plucks the feathers off chickens at the Tyson factory? If he makes a mistake, no one hears about it. One of the most basic truths about leadership is that the more visible you are and the higher your position, the more people will know—and have an opinion—about your mistakes.

Here is the principle: *With responsibility comes visibility and accountability.* If you want more responsibility, you must be willing to accept visibility and accountability. That's true whether you're a leader in government, business, school, or church. The higher you move up the leadership ladder, the greater your visibility and the more people will know about your mistakes.

With that increased responsibility and visibility comes greater accountability. Since more people know about your mistakes, you're accountable to more people. The president is accountable to hundreds of millions of people! In leadership, that's part of the deal. If you want responsibility, don't whine about visibility and accountability. If you don't want to be accountable and you can't handle the visibility, step off the leadership ladder. You don't get one without the other.

Yes, we all make mistakes, but leaders need to consider carefully how they handle those mistakes. To help us learn how to do this well, I've created categories of mistakes. Before we begin, I want to remind you that in general we're talking here about mistakes, not sins. Some mistakes are sin, but not all of them.

Categories of Mistakes

You forget to do something you said you would do.

This is a common mistake. You told someone on your team that you'd call them on Monday, but you forgot. You said, "I've got it handled" when you didn't. People will usually cut you slack the first time this happens, even the second time, but if you continue to forget and don't carry through on your responsibilities, this diminishes the trust between you and the other person.

I worked with a team member who repeatedly gave the same answer when asked about an assignment: "No problem. I've got it in focus. It's covered." But it wasn't. The research wasn't done. The room wasn't ready. The people weren't informed. The job wasn't finished. After a while, I began to doubt not only his ability, but also his integrity.

When trust is diminished, people no longer accept your excuses at face value; instead, they investigate. They ask more questions and simple requests become complex with multiple layers of documentation. People expect immediate follow-up and assume you aren't going to keep your word.

You mistakenly do something wrong.

This isn't the same as forgetting to do something. It's about attempting to carry out a responsibility but messing up. You attached the wrong pieces to each other, you broke the remote, you ruined the file. Remember, we aren't talking about intentional mistakes here but completely unintentional mistakes.

Years ago, one of our team members made a mistake when counting a special offering. With great celebration, I told the missionary the amount of funds involved. Two days later, I discovered the actual amount. The total reported to me was over $50,000 more than the actual total! I had already given my word to the missionary, so with a big gulp, I wrote the check for the larger amount. That mistake wasn't malicious or evil, it was just a mistake. But, it was an expensive one! Afterward, a member of our management team asked if I was going to fire the team member who had made the mistake. My reply was, "Absolutely not! Why would I want to waste a high-dollar lesson? She'll never make that mistake, or one like it, again. She's more valuable now than she was last week!"

My thought is that we're probably way too hard on ourselves and others when we make mistakes. You may have heard the saying: "Never lose. Either win or learn." I think we can apply this same mentality to mistakes in our lives. Personally, it doesn't bother me when people make mistakes when their efforts are in earnest and the experience moves them forward.

You have a bad attitude.

Once you have more than one person in a room, you're bound to experience attitude mistakes. These types of mistakes happen more often among the immature. We don't fault a two-year-old child for a bad attitude when someone takes their toy—they're learning how to control their emotions and get along with others.

But if a twenty-two-year old throws a fit when they don't get their way? Everyone within range of the incident cringes inwardly. That young man or woman is supposed to be more mature.

If a fifty-two-year old has a temper tantrum when someone doesn't do what they want, they have a major problem.

As you mature, you should make fewer attitude mistakes, not more. If you see someone who makes a lot of attitude mistakes, they're immature—both emotionally and spiritually.

Once you have more than one person in a room, you're bound to experience attitude mistakes.

This is a big focus area for me. Although I manage the outward projection of my feelings well, I still struggle with my attitude. After much trial and error, I've learned that I need to carefully monitor my attitude when dealing with problem people. No matter what others do, even if they're rude and mean and wrong, I get to pick my attitude towards them. No one else can control my attitude. If I allow their wrong to determine my attitude, I've given them control over me. No one can make me have a bad attitude! My attitude is my choice.

You violate core values.

No doubt you operate with basic core values in your business, your family, your church, or other organization. Hopefully, you've determined your personal core values.

Any time you violate a core value, it's a mistake. One of the core values of our church is "Everything is better in teams." That's foundational to everything we do. Years ago one of our pastors was responsible to put up the Christmas lights around our property. Rather than organize a team to help, he decided to do it himself. Was that a sin? No, but it was a big mistake. Why? He had violated one of our core values. Not only that, but he got stuck up in the air on a lift with no one around to rescue him!

Core values serve as a compass for the organization. We've all agreed on those values and agree to let them influence our actions, words, and decisions. When someone violates a core value, it creates dissonance. When what we do is different from what we say, people begin to doubt our motives as well as our integrity.

To help you understand a little better, here are the core values at our church, First Assembly:

- Every soul matters to God.
- Everything is better in teams.
- We resolve conflict biblically.
- The Bible is our guidebook for living.
- We must build healthy families.
- We connect with God through worship and prayer.

I can assure you that we cannot and will not violate those values!

You mess up with people.

There are several categories of people-mistakes, but one of the costliest is hiring the wrong person or putting the wrong person in leadership. When you feel desperate to fill a position, you may act too quickly. Then you're stuck with a team member who doesn't fit the team or the role.

This happens often in churches. You feel the pressure to find a worship leader. You're worried about going too long without one, so you choose someone for the role based on their ability and neglect to determine their character. That quick leadership decision can create heartache for you and the church.

My mentor Alton Garrison tells me often, "It's easier to anoint someone that to 'un-anoint' someone." Be slow to hire. Don't get in a hurry. Make sure the person you are considering is the right fit before you assign the position. The momentary hardships caused by a vacant position pale in comparison to the heartache of having the wrong person in place. It's better to have no one than the wrong one!

Another common people-mistake is missing the chance to connect with someone—to affirm or encourage them. Last December my schedule was crushing. I had more than thirty Christmas parties to attend, ten extra nights of rehearsal for special services, and multiple big events. In the middle of it all, I completely forgot to attend one party. I was in the same building and the event was on my calendar, but I didn't go. With such a packed schedule, you might think I was justified in missing that party—and if events like that were merely check boxes on my task list, I might agree with you. But it wasn't the event I regretted missing as much as the opportunity to connect with a group of people who needed my encouragement.

I often remind our team, "Walk slowly through the halls. We should never be too busy for people! If you must run or rush, go outside where no one can see you. Never miss the chance to love people."

The final common people-mistake is trusting someone you never should have trusted. You overlooked a pattern of broken relationships in their past and decided this time would be different. Then, the person betrays your trust. That's difficult and painful. I've been there. I've suffered the sting of betrayal; however, rather than blame the person, I reminded myself, "I chose that person. It's my fault." I wasn't trying to beat myself up. I simply wanted to own the mistake so I wouldn't repeat it!

You make financial mistakes.

You spend when you should save. You buy things with a credit card when you should wait to pay cash. You purchase something you don't need. Financial mistakes are expensive and embarrassing!

You violate Scripture.

Although some mistakes are also sin, many mistakes are not sin. However, when you violate Scripture, you don't simply make a mistake, you sin. It's important not to diminish sin by referring to it as a mistake. "Everyone who sins is breaking God's law, for all sin is contrary to the law of God" (1 John 3:4, NLT).

- Sexual sin is exactly that—sin. It isn't just a mistake.
- Taking the Lord's name in vain is a mistake, but it's also sin.
- Gossip is a mistake. It's also sin.

When your reaction to sin is the same as your reaction to a mistake, this creates separation between you and God.

Typical Ways People Manage Mistakes

There are many more categories of mistakes we could list. You may have thought of several yourself. But let's turn our attention now to consider some typical ways people try to manage mistakes. As you read through the common reactions, remember they also apply to sin.

They hide it.

You cover it up and hope it's never discovered. The thought here is, *If no one knows about it, then it's not really a mistake.* But, inevitably, the cover-up becomes an ever-increasing cycle of mistakes.

Hiding a mistake is the way children handle things. It's funny when they do it. They say things like, "I don't know how the TV screen got broken. I don't know where that golf ball came from. I didn't do it." The Internet is filled with hilarious clips of kids blaming their siblings or making up elaborate stories about their mistakes.

Hiding a mistake is the way children handle things.

We laugh when kids do this, but it's not so funny when adults do it. Some people will go to amazing lengths to cover up their mistakes. Then, when the mistake is finally discovered, they're more sharply criticized for the cover-up than for the original mistake!

They go into "scramble mode."

"Scramble mode" is my invented term. It's kind of hard to describe, but you know it when you see it. Someone in scramble mode tries to bluff so you won't realize they made a mistake.

Someone in scramble mode attempts a quick fix. They realize: "Oops! I shouldn't have done that! I shouldn't have said that. I've got to fix it before anyone sees it. I know what to do, I'll . . ." What comes next is often a humorous, poor attempt at covering the truth.

Sometimes I send someone an e-mail and ask, "Did you finish that for me?" The person responds, "Just finishing it. I'll e-mail it to you in about fifteen minutes." When I get it, I know they spent exactly fifteen minutes on it, frantically cutting and pasting from some other document or website. They were in scramble mode.

They lie.

Sadly, this is often what people do to manage their mistakes. They lie, hoping they won't get caught. But, when they lie, their mistake is now compounded by sin.

> **If you blame your mistakes on someone or something else, you won't learn from your mistakes and are doomed to repeat them.**

When they do get caught, they still don't tell the whole truth. People who lie to cover a mistake will only reveal the truth in stages. They tell you the minimum amount of truth they think will resolve the situation. As you keep asking more questions, and time goes on, you find out more and more of the truth.

Ultimately everyone knows the truth, and the lie is revealed. When you lie to cover a mistake you not only mess up, you also lose trust.

They blame it on someone or something else.

The number one enemy of growth is blame. If you blame your mistakes on someone or something else, you won't learn from your mistakes and are doomed to repeat them. That's why I caution parents that one of the worst mistakes they can make is to teach their children that errors and mistakes are always someone else's fault:

- Bad grades? Bad teacher.
- Got in trouble at church? The pastor doesn't like you.
- Relationship difficulties? The other person has a problem.

When you blame someone else for your problems, you avoid dealing with your personal issues, confessing your sins, and finding forgiveness—and it's not just children who struggle with this.

- Your unhappy marriage? All your spouse's fault.
- Your second unhappy marriage? Again, spouse's fault.
- Keep losing jobs? Employer's fault, every time.
- Children not living right? It's the church's fault, the youth pastor's fault, or the school's fault.

People fix the blame on others to avoid dealing with their own issues. As long as they can blame someone else, they can hide from the pain of personal failure.

If you do that long enough, you can even deceive yourself. You can believe that it's all the fault of other people. I have a friend like that. Each time he gets a new job, he starts wonderfully. Then something goes wrong. He has a whole list of people to blame for his failure. In each situation, he truly believes it's their fault. He's never made the connection that he's the only thing all those places have in common! You'll never grow up until you tell yourself the truth!

They make excuses.

One week in staff meeting I asked our team to give me the top ten excuses people give for their business or church not reaching its potential. The answers came quickly:

- We're a small church.
- It's a small town.
- No one wants to work.
- These people are lazy.
- I didn't know that wouldn't work.
- The denomination should give us more help.
- Everyone is against me.
- These people don't know what they're doing.
- No one is willing to follow me.
- I need more money, space, or resources.

Making excuses doesn't do anything to fix problems or mistakes—it just makes leaders look bad.

A pattern of making excuses has a similar effect to the mistake of forgetting to do what you said you would do. People may accept an excuse the first few times, but ultimately, they'll begin to doubt your word. Doubts inevitably lead to an investigation of the truth, and when the truth is discovered, trust erodes quickly. Once your credibility is damaged in this way, people will no longer believe your excuses—or much else you say for that matter.

They draw attention to someone else's mistake—deflection.

This is a classic tool of children. When you challenge their report card, they say: "Sure, I got a C in history, but wait until you see my sister's report card!"

In adults it sounds like this:

Making excuses doesn't do anything to fix problems or mistakes—it just makes leaders look bad.

- I might have looked at pornography, but at least I didn't have an affair like _____.

- Well, maybe I messed up, but look at what you did.

- I might not have done it right, but at least I didn't do what Bob did!

- I haven't been sensitive to her needs, but you wait until you hear what she called me.

- Maybe I shouldn't have bought this, but at least I didn't max out my credit card like she did.

- I was a little late to work, but I know I'll put in a better day in these seven hours than anyone else will.

- I know I've put on some weight, but I'm in a lot better shape than most people my age.

You get caught making a mistake so you look for someone else who's made a mistake—preferably a bigger mistake—to deflect the attention to them. Some people are especially talented at this. They do it with a little humor, reminding you of someone else's failures in a subtle way.

I hate this method of dealing with mistakes. My answer is always, "We're not talking about them. We're talking about *you*. I can't help them, but you're right here in front of me. Let's talk about what *you* can do differently."

When people who have messed up attack me for my mistakes, I know we're dealing with a bigger issue. It's not about me at all.

They tell a "technical truth."

What's a technical truth? It's when you aren't technically lying, but your words are constructed in a manner to intentionally lead the person to believe something other than what is true.

One of my staff members has a precocious (and precious!) eight-year-old daughter who, after being told to take a shower, emerged from the bathroom with completely dry hair. When questioned about this phenomenon, the little girl adamantly replied that she had, in fact, taken a shower. After several exchanges, her mom finally asked, "Did you wash your hair with shampoo and wash your body with soap?" Suddenly, the truth came out: The little girl had spent fifteen minutes letting the hot water run—without washing at all!

Trust is best earned and learned in the context of mistakes.

Did the girl technically tell the truth? Yes. But her technical truth was intended to lead her parents to believe she had obeyed completely when she had not. A "technical truth" told by an eight-year-old generally doesn't have long-lasting consequences; nevertheless, a technical truth is a lie. As you grow in maturity and influence, the repercussions of a lie grow as well. Like lies, technical truths will cost you respect and, ultimately, will damage your integrity.

The Right Way to Manage Mistakes

Regardless of which method you choose to skirt around a mistake, anything short of facing it head-on erodes confidence in your leadership and can cost you the trust of your team. It's a paradox, but trust is best earned and learned in the context of mistakes.

Mistakes are a crucible for revealing character. You see, the best time for you to learn about my nature is when you mess up. How I deal with your mistake indicates how much value I place on you and our relationship.

When is my character revealed? When I don't get my way. When I disagree. When I make a mistake. The way I manage these things reveals the depths of my character.

Thankfully, there's a right way to manage mistakes. Regardless of the nature of your mistake, here's the pattern to follow.

Step 1: Admit it.

When I was growing up my parents had a rule about wrong behavior: "If you tell on yourself, you won't get punished. But if we hear about it from someone else, you're in big trouble." When I messed up, I'd race home to tell on myself before my sister or anyone else could report me. It's a good thing to learn. Admit your mistake! Chances are people already know about it or will soon know anyway. Demonstrate your character by admitting your mistake.

You may think you successfully hid it, but you didn't. That's the worst thing! The person who knows your mistake and the fact that you hid it loses respect for you. I often ask questions I already know the answers to. Why? I want to see how people respond . . . what they admit. I want to discover their character.

Admitting your mistakes is a biblical principle. It's called confession. "Confess your sins to each other and pray for each other so that you may be healed" (James 5:16, NLT). "Whoever conceals their sins does not prosper, but the one who confesses and renounces them finds mercy" (Proverbs 28:13).

A few years ago, we did a big Halloween event at our church. We called it Candy Factory. We turned every room in our facility into part of the factory. Each ministry group created their own space. It was amazing! We had conveyor belts, chocolate machines, and more candy than a Walmart!

The problem was, it was a little too amazing. I knew we were in trouble when I looked outside ninety minutes before the event and the line of people was a half-mile long. Things only got worse. By sixty minutes into the event, our goal had changed: No longer were we trying to connect with people; we were simply trying to keep someone from being trampled!

Afterward, our building was an absolute disaster! It took our entire team and a huge group of volunteers a whole week to clean and restore the building to its former state.

The next Sunday night I stood in front of the church and said, "How many of you were at Candy Factory?" After a bit of nervous laughter, almost every hand went up. Everyone wondered what I was going to say next.

I said, "I want to tell you, I'm sorry. That event was a

disaster—the worst thing we've ever done. I promise you, we'll never do that again!"

The crowd gave me a standing ovation. Everyone knew the event was a mistake-filled disaster. When I admitted it, the crowd immediately forgave me. We moved on and didn't talk about it again. Now, years later, we are finally able to laugh about it!

Step 2: Own it.

If it's your mistake, you get to "own" it. Don't make excuses. Just simply own your mistake. Do like I did after the Candy Factory disaster. Say, "I did it, and I'm sorry." Likely, everyone already knows it was your mistake. Owning it opens the door for forgiveness, which enables everyone to move on. Resist the impulse to blame other people. Own it.

If it's your mistake, you get to "own" it.

Paul wrote, "Each one should test their own actions. Then they can take pride in themselves alone, without comparing themselves to someone else, for each one should carry their own load" (Galatians 6:4–5). Carry your own load. Own your own mistakes. It may surprise you, but the vulnerability you offer in those moments increases your credibility with your followers! That kind of vulnerability also enables and empowers your followers to claim responsibility for their own mistakes in the future. You have shown them how to do it.

Step 3: Fix it.

If you make the mistake, the damage-control responsibility is yours. Accept the consequences yourself rather than pass them on. You must do whatever it takes to correct the mistake.

This is one of my biggest frustrations as a leader. Someone makes a mistake, then expects me to fix it. They leave it in my lap and expect me to handle it. Leadership doesn't work that way.

Once when my son Tyler was new to our pastoral staff, he made the mistake of offhandedly telling the crowd that as part of our Easter weekend celebration we would have ushers at the doors with Mountain Dews so everyone would be energized for our earliest Sunday morning service. When he returned from the pulpit I politely informed him that the church had not planned to purchase Mountain Dews for Easter Sunday, nor would it. But because Tyler had made the announcement, he had to make good on his word. The week before Easter he went to the local big-box store and purchased—with his own money—sodas for all the early risers at First Assembly. Unfortunately, that announcement was Tyler's mistake, and the consequences were his as well.

- If you promised Mountain Dews, you buy them.
- If you broke it, you apologize.
- If you gave the wrong instructions, you fix things the right way.
- If you offered an incorrect appointment time, you adjust your schedule to accommodate.
- If it's your mistake, you fix it!

Step 4: Make it right.

Making it right goes beyond simply fixing the problem. Making it right means you make reparation for the negative consequences or damages you've caused. If someone else had to cover for you, or your mistake hurt that person, do whatever it takes to make amends. If you lied, go back and tell the truth. If you broke it, replace it. If you lost it, buy another one. If you hurt someone's feelings, apologize.

There are three components to an effective apology:

- *I'm sorry.* Admit it.
- *I was wrong.* Own it.
- *What can I do to make it right?* Make amends.

When you make amends, do more than the minimum. Return what you took . . . and then some! Make it right and more.

Step 5: Study it.

This is the step most people skip. Study your mistake. Ask yourself: *Why did I do that? Is it a pattern? Do I often handle this kind of situation or person in the wrong way? How can I avoid repeating that mistake?*

You might say, "Rod, that sounds depressing! Why would I want to think about my mistake?" Simple—so you don't repeat it! Studying your mistake helps you identify motives, patterns, and bad habits so you can intentionally change and avoid making a similar mistake in the future. What you don't study, you're bound to repeat!

As a church, we evaluate everything. We carefully study our mistakes because we want to learn from them! This is God's way of educating us. "God's correction is always right and for our best good, that we may share his holiness. Being punished isn't enjoyable while it is happening—it hurts! But afterwards we can see the result, a quiet growth in grace and character" (Hebrews 12:10–11, TLB).

Step 6: Don't repeat it!

I've only been a senior pastor for sixteen years. I'm going to keep making mistakes. I just want to make different ones. I don't want to make the same one again.

Repeating the same mistake is called a "pattern." A pattern brings into question one of two things: competency or character. When people question your competency, they wonder if you have what it takes to get the job done. They doubt your intelligence or ability. When people question your character, they don't think you made a mistake. They see your pattern as an intentional decision-making process. Either one is bad for a leader!

Step 7: Seek forgiveness.

Seek forgiveness from people. Go to them and say, "I'm sorry. I was wrong. Would you forgive me? What can I do to make it right?"

If your mistake was sin, seek forgiveness from God. "If we confess our sins, he is faithful and just and will forgive us our sins and purify us from all unrighteousness" (1 John 1:9).

Your mistakes don't have to follow you forever. You can be forgiven, restored, and still accomplish everything God planned for you.

Stuff to consider . . .

1. Brainstorm a list of your most epic fails and study the list. (If you're working with your team, be sure to choose the ones that are far enough behind you that you can laugh about them now; choosing recent mistakes could put salt in fresh wounds!)

2. What are the greatest lessons you've learned from your mistakes?

3. Do you see a pattern in your mistakes?

4. Do you mishandle a certain type of situation or person often?

5. How can you avoid repeating that mistake?

4

Unresolved Conflict Never Solved Anything

I answered my phone and heard a voice shaking with emotion. It was Jackson, a staff member at a large church in another state, asking for my advice. He had conflicted with the executive leadership team at that church over a series of his decisions.

By the time I got involved, the participants had called their lawyers, were threatening lawsuits, and had made character assassinations. It was ugly . . . and getting uglier. I read all the documents, attended lengthy meetings, and tried to help them negotiate to resolve the conflict. I knew reconciliation wasn't likely but hoped for at least a friendly parting. Sadly, that didn't happen. They burned the bridge, broke the relationship, and hurt innocent people in the process.

A few months later, I watched another conflict develop. It started rather innocently. Ezra and Rachael threw a party and invited everyone involved in their ministry area, except for Samuel and Beth. Samuel and Beth got mad! They posted on Facebook and started calling people to rally against Ezra and Rachael. Before long, people were angry and threatening physical violence. Ezra and Rachael maintained it was their right to invite whomever they wanted. Samuel and Beth were convinced it was part of a bigger strategy to force them out of the church. Both sides were in the wrong, but neither side was willing to budge an inch. Eventually the incident tore that church apart and the former friends still won't speak to each other.

I believe conflict should be resolved—and I believe all conflict can be resolved. But is all conflict resolved? Of course not! Not in this world, and sadly, not in the body of Christ. If we followed scriptural principles we would resolve all conflict.

When you resolve a conflict with another person, it doesn't mean you become best friends, still work together, or call each other every week; it does mean the incident no longer boils in your spirit. You can think of that person without bitterness, anger, or hate. You can move beyond the hurt and the angry emotions.

Paul addressed this issue with the church in Colossae:

> Therefore, as God's chosen people, holy and dearly loved, clothe yourselves with compassion, kindness, humility, gentleness and patience. Bear with each other and forgive one another if any of you has a grievance against someone. Forgive as the Lord forgave you. And over all these virtues put on love, which binds them all together in perfect unity.
>
> Let the peace of Christ rule in your hearts, since as members of one body you were called to peace. And be thankful. (Colossians 3:12-15)

In the body of Christ, unresolved conflict grieves the heart of God and discredits our testimony. We should resolve all conflict in the body of Christ! At the very least, we can agree to disagree, within the bond of unity and love.

From the conflicts I've observed, I've developed a set of principles to manage and resolve conflict. Whether you're personally involved in the conflict or simply helping others resolve conflict, if you put these principles into practice you can resolve it in a healthy way.

Principles to Manage and Resolve Conflict

Focus on making it right, not on being right.

What's the difference between "being right" and "making it right"? Being right is about me. I care most about what I want, what I need, and what will make me happy. Conversely, making it right is about God's kingdom. The goal changes from what is best for me to what is best for others. What matters most for the body of Christ is advancing the cause of Christ and furthering His purpose.

> **What matters most for the body of Christ is advancing the cause of Christ and furthering His purpose.**

Being right is driven by pride. Your ego, your reputation, and your recognition are at stake. When your focus is on being right, you put yourself first and up front. A focus on making it right requires humility. The goal is not to advance yourself but to put others first. The key phrase in humility is, "Others first, me last."

Being right is all about winning. You might recognize this in someone close to you who must always be right. They turn everything into a competition. Their goal is to have the last word, and prove they're right and you're wrong. A person focused on winning is defensive. They're convinced that if they give any ground, they won't be the winner. They want to convince as many people as possible to join their side. It's sad, but the person who must always win, loses. People get tired of the competition and drop out of the battle, the argument, the relationship, the friendship, or the marriage. The cost of winning is lost relationships.

Let's be realistic. Chances are at least part of the problem is yours.

Making it right is about continuing in relationship. This person's approach is different. Their mind-set is, "I may not win every point, but I want to be in relationship with you. Relationship matters more than competing or winning." In the conflicts I mentioned earlier, both sides were focused on winning. As a result, they destroyed the relationships.

Being right is concerned with saving face and managing reputation. The main concern is, "How will people see me? What will people think about me?" A person obsessed with being right doesn't want people to know they've made a mistake, so they do whatever it takes to prove they're right to maintain their image.

The goal of making it right is to move forward. Because this person knows their identity is in Christ and is not determined by people or circumstances, they can say, "There's a lot at stake here. We can't afford to fight with each other. I don't have to be right. You don't have to be right. Let's make it right, get back on mission, and move forward."

The person who wants to be right worries what others think and makes sure others know they're right! It's a selfish way to approach conflict . . . and life.

On the other hand, the person who wants to make it right worries what God thinks. If your focus is making it right, you want to stand before God with a clean heart, knowing you promoted unity in His body.

Apologize. Accept responsibility for your part of the problem.

In both conflicts I mentioned earlier neither side was willing to admit any wrong. Both parties believed that the other person was entirely wrong while they were entirely right. That attitude never resolves conflict.

Often when someone comes for counseling, they don't want to talk about their side of the issue. In fact, they don't believe they have a side in the issue! The whole problem is the other person's fault. I'm quite unpopular in counseling because I don't want to talk about what the other person did. I want to talk about what *you* did so I can help you discover your part of the problem.

Wow! You should read the e-mails I get from people who didn't want to hear about their part of the problem. They make it my problem that they don't want to address their problem while they're focusing on someone else's problem. They certainly don't return to me for counseling!

Let's be realistic. Chances are at least part of the problem is yours. Realistically assess how you could have handled the situation differently. Then, be quick to apologize and restore the relationship.

If you have a problem with a brother or sister, deal with it now. Don't wait for later. Put down this book and go to them. Don't allow anger and resentment to simmer. Find a way to resolve the issue before it becomes bigger. "Do not let the sun go down while you are still angry, and do not give the devil a foothold" (Ephesians 4:26–27).

You might say, "Wait a minute. It wasn't all my fault." I understand that. Go first anyway. Don't give the devil a foothold. Apologize for what was your fault.

By the way, if the word "if" is in your apology, that's not an apology. "I'm sorry if I offended you" is a clever way of saying, "You're immature and shouldn't have been offended." Instead say, "I'm sorry I offended you." If that person wasn't offended, they'll let you know.

Keep the conflict to yourself.

The number one mistake I see in response to conflict is people share the story. They present their case over and over and involve other people. That's the exact opposite of Jesus' instructions! "If your brother or sister sins, go and point out their fault, just between the two of you" (Matthew 18:15).

According to Jesus, the first step in conflict resolution is to go to the person one-on-one, talk through it, and resolve the issue. Sadly, with the popularity of social media, that seems to happen less and less. Instead of going to the person you have a problem with, you post an angry rant and invite others to join in your anger. I've watched preachers do this. Rather than follow the biblical pattern, they seek to gain an audience by publicly airing their grievances with another minister or church. If you ask them about this, they have "good" reasons to talk to other people, but even "good" reasons aren't an excuse for ignoring scriptural commands. "Don't speak evil against each other, dear brothers and sisters. If you criticize and judge each other, then you are criticizing and judging God's law. But your job is to obey the law, not to judge whether it applies to you" (James 4:11, NLT).

I understand; you want to build your case. You want to be sure people hear your side of the story. You want to make sure you win. But not only is this sin, it's also a bad conflict-resolution strategy.

When you go public with a conflict, the situation escalates. It doesn't get better; it gets worse as more people get involved. In the case of Samuel and Beth, rather than keep the conflict with Ezra and Rachael to themselves, they shared their side loudly and publicly. The results were disastrous as people chose sides and friends became enemies.

> **When you go public with a conflict, the situation escalates.**

When you share your conflict with others one of three things can happen:

- *They can agree with you.* Although that seems like a win, it's not. Now, you've drawn them into your dysfunctional pattern and your sin. They become part of the conflict.
- *They can disagree with you.* Suddenly, instead of having one conflict you have many conflicts.
- *They can confront your sin.* That doesn't happen very often, but it's the right response. Why doesn't it happen? People know if you're eager to talk to them about someone, you'll be just as eager to talk to someone else about them, so they decide to avoid the issue rather than confront it.

When you go public, other people pick up your offense—especially children and spouses. I hear stories all the time from people who are mad at the church for something that happened (or supposedly happened) to someone else. The problem is, when people pick up your offense they don't automatically pick up your forgiveness.

Believe the best of others. Be patient and give others the benefit of the doubt.

When you go public with your grievances, you also make it difficult to back off your statements. If you keep the conflict between you and the other person, you can change your mind and give in. But, when you tell others, you make it much more difficult to have a change of heart.

Give others the benefit of the doubt.

It's interesting. We want other people to give us the benefit of the doubt. "After all, they know I wouldn't do that. I'm not that way." We want the benefit of the doubt, but we're not always as willing to give others the benefit of the doubt.

Several weeks ago, someone confronted me. They said, "You ignored me in the hallway last Sunday morning." That Sunday morning I had attended a meeting, preached three times, greeted people at the door three times, met people in the Guest Center four times, and had lunch with several families new to our church. Is it possible—as a finite human being—I might have innocently missed someone in the hallway on the way to my next responsibility? Rather than consider that and give me the benefit of the doubt, that person automatically assumed I had purposely ignored them. The truth is, I simply hadn't seen them!

Instead of assuming the worst, assume that person's motive wasn't to hurt or harm you. Ask yourself: *Is it possible they didn't mean it? What's their character? What's their track record?* Assume the best of others. It takes so much pressure off when you assume good instead of evil. "Always be humble and gentle. Be patient with each other, making allowance for each other's faults because of your love. Make every effort to keep yourselves united in the Spirit, binding yourselves together with peace" (Ephesians 4:2–3, NLT).

Believe the best of others. Be patient and give others the benefit of the doubt. When you do that, you promote peace.

Control your emotions.

Anger causes you to do things you later regret. If you can't have a confrontation without yelling, don't have it. When you lose your temper, you lose. People will never forget the words you yell in a fit of rage.

Don't walk out of a room or a meeting in anger. "I'm mad and I'm leaving" is incredibly immature. When you do that, you're like a child on the playground who says, "Fine. If you won't play by my rules, I'm going to take my ball and go home." Act like a mature adult. Control yourself.

Your excuse may be, "You should see what they did to me." I'm not talking about them. I'm talking about you. Why would you allow their wrong to be your excuse to do wrong?

Stick to the facts.

When you're trying to resolve a conflict, you'll probably have a lot of strong feelings and opinions. In that moment, even though you think you know the right thing to do—and especially what the other person should do!—only discuss what you know to be *true*.

Margaret came into my office. Her face was red, and her voice loud. She was so upset I couldn't figure out what she was talking about. Finally, when she slowed down, I interrupted with a question. "Margaret, what in the world has you so upset?" With a lot of emotion she explained that Bruce had told everyone she was causing problems. When I asked if she'd heard Bruce say that, she confessed she hadn't personally heard it, but "someone had told her he had said it." I looked at her and said, "Margaret, let me get this straight. You're upset about something Bruce said. But, you didn't hear him say it, and you can't even remember who told you they heard him say it. What if Bruce didn't say it?"

We decided to find out. As it turned out, Bruce *didn't* say it. And the person who reported it to Margaret hadn't said that he had said it. Margaret was angry at something Bruce hadn't said. In fact, Bruce said the opposite: Margaret was helping to solve a problem.

Stick to the facts! Don't confront someone based on what you think they said or what someone else reported they said. Don't overreact to statements made by people who want to stir things up.

I'm going to help you by giving you a glossary of terms troublemakers often use, along the correct definition:

> *"Everybody is angry with you."*— "I've convinced three of my friends to join me in my anger."
> *"Everybody is talking about it."* — "I've told everyone I can."
> *"Nobody likes you."* — "I don't like you."
> *"All my friends agree with me."* — "Both of my friends feel the same way."

"Let me tell you so you can pray about it." — (I don't need to interpret that one.)

"Bless her heart." — "She's an idiot."

"Do you have a minute?" — "I'm about to destroy the next hour for you."

"I'm not trying to be negative." — "I don't have to try. It comes naturally."

People add imaginary "others" who support their argument to make it seem stronger. Any time you hear that others are involved, chances are good no one else is talking about it and no one else is upset. If a lot of people felt that way, you'd already have heard about it. You're likely dealing with someone who is dysfunctional in conflict resolution and knows their position is weak.

When people tell me, "A lot of people," I stop them and ask, "Okay, exactly who? Can you give me some names? Where are they? Let's bring them in here before we continue talking. You don't have to speak for them. Invite them all. Is my office big enough, or do we need to move to the sanctuary to have enough space for them all?" They quickly back off the statement that "a lot of people feel this way."

Don't overreact. Keep things in perspective.

In the old days, they said it this way: "Don't make a mountain out of a molehill." Don't take something little and turn it into a major deal.

Someone forgot to invite you to the party. Don't turn that into, "They don't want me around. They're against me. They hate me and are turning everyone against me." No. Chances are, they just forgot.

Don't overreact. Your response should fit the offense. If it's a small thing, keep your response small. Don't make the situation bigger than it is.

When you overreact, you say things like:

"Everyone is angry with me."
"Nobody likes me."
"You always do that."

Words like *always, everyone, nobody,* and *never* are classic examples of overreaction. Keep things in perspective. Don't leap to a conclusion until you have all the information. Matter of fact, that's a biblical principle:

> I have used Apollos and myself to illustrate what I've been saying. If you pay attention to what I have quoted from the Scriptures, you won't be proud of one of your leaders at the expense of another. (1 Corinthians 4:6, NLT)

Find common ground.

There's almost always common ground between the parties involved in a conflict. Do your best to find it. In the conflict I tried to resolve between Jackson and the church leadership team, I decided to assume that both sides were people who loved the Lord. Once I assumed that, I was able to find the proper response. We were able to reach a peaceful solution over the one thing everyone agreed on: They all loved the Lord.

If you can't find common ground, you're likely dealing with someone who is a sinner in need of a Savior. Wait . . . you were once a sinner, weren't you? That becomes your common ground. There's always common ground because

> Together as one body, Christ reconciled both groups to God by means of his death on the cross, and our hostility toward each other was put to death.

> He brought this Good News of peace to you Gentiles who were far away from him, and peace to the Jews who were near. Now all of us can come to the Father through the same Holy Spirit because of what Christ has done for us. (Ephesians 2:16–18, NLT)

Seek resolution, not punishment or pain.

Don't pile on! Too many times the conflict continues because one person wants to make sure the other person pays for what they did. They want to make sure that person gets what they deserve. Remember, the goal is to resolve the conflict—not punish the offender. Listen to the instructions of Paul as he addressed a conflict in the Early Church:

> Remember that the man I wrote about, who caused all the trouble, has not caused sorrow to me as much as to all the rest of you—though I certainly have my share in it too. I don't want to be harder on him than I should. He has been punished enough by your united disapproval. Now it is time to forgive him and comfort him.

Otherwise he may become so bitter and discouraged that he won't be able to recover. Please show him now that you still do love him very much. (2 Corinthians 2:5-8, TLB)

Years ago, one of my best friends did me a great wrong. The things he said and did were unbelievable. The lies he told were ridiculous. Through it all, I was quiet. I never joined the fight, but instead decided to let my life and reputation stand for itself.

One Sunday night the man who told the lies came back to church. Several of our board members came to me and said, "James is here. What are you doing to do? Do you want us to tell him to leave?"

I said, "No! He can stay. I've forgiven him. I'm going to help him get back on his feet and pour on the love because that's what the Bible says to do. I don't have a choice."

You might be thinking, *That's easy for you to say, but you don't know how badly someone hurt me.* Will hurting your offender make you feel better? If so, then you have an issue with forgiveness. What's more, your heart isn't aligned with the heart of God, who—thankfully—doesn't take that approach. Our sin puts us in conflict with God, yet His focus isn't on punishment but resolution. He sent His Son to die on a cross to resolve the conflict of sin, and He calls us to follow His example "as dearly loved children and [to] walk in the way of love, just as Christ loved us and gave himself up for us" (Ephesians 5:1–2). While God would have been justified in heaping punishment upon us, He forgave. We should do the same.

Do what's right.

Regardless of the intensity of the conflict or the evil someone else has done to you, keep doing what's right. No wrong on the other person's part justifies sin on your part. No matter what they do, determine to do right. Evil may overcome good for a time, but ultimately, right always wins! Keep doing right. You aren't responsible for the other person's actions or words. You're responsible for *your* words and actions. It doesn't matter what they do. You do right.

> **You aren't responsible for the other person's actions or words. You're responsible for *your* words and actions.**

I've learned a simple fact: You can't have a conflict unless two people are involved. All you need to do is refuse to be involved. Drop out of the competition. Let it be their issue and their issue alone. Don't fight, just do right. Right will ultimately prevail.

Guard the hearts and spirits of the people closest to you.

In conflict, don't just guard your heart, guard the hearts of others. In an escalated conflict, be particularly aware of those closest to you—your spouse, children, and closest friends. Be careful not to infect their spirits with your ill feelings.

Wouldn't it be horrible if your unresolved conflict and your harsh words caused your children to turn their backs on God? Wouldn't it be tragic if your gossiping mouth kept your husband from a relationship with Christ? Guard the hearts of others! Don't risk someone else paying the price for your conflict.

My friend James came back to church. Although we never returned to being best friends, we resolved our conflict. Sadly, James' children never got over it. They remain angry at me, at church, and at God. James included them in his anger, but wasn't able to include them in his healing. James is heartbroken at the price his family has paid for his sin. I still pray for them to find healing and return to faith.

Learn your lesson.

Most people have a pattern in their relational conflicts. The same type of issue crops up repeatedly. Someone causes a problem in church, and you discover they also caused a similar problem in the last church they attended. Another person has the same problem in their third marriage that they had in their first and second marriages.

Study your conflict to learn important lessons. Discover the pattern of your conflicts and determine to resolve it—don't repeat the same mistakes! Learn your lesson! Too often we're focused on the other person learning their lesson, but we neglect to learn our own.

That's another reason people don't like to talk to me about their conflict. I start probing. I want to know: "Is this the first time something like this has happened? Is there a pattern in your life? Have you had the same issue with others? If so, let's talk about *your* problem!"

How to Know Which Person Is in the Right

In my various roles, I have the responsibility of being a mediator and helping others resolve conflict on a regular basis. I've developed a grid to help me evaluate which side of the conflict is in the right. It's not completely foolproof, but these five questions will help you assess responsibility.

- *Who is attacking?* The person attacking is almost always the person who in the wrong.

- *Who is following the biblical model?* Is one side attempting to involve others in the conflict? Is either side attempting to resolve the conflict directly, according to Jesus' instructions?

- *Whose track record is good?* Conflict seems to follow some people wherever they go, but they always have a story about how it was the other person's fault. Pay attention to their track record. If Tim has a problem with Patrick . . . and Tim has a problem with James . . . and Tim has a problem with Joe . . . and Tim has a problem with John . . . guess what? Tim is likely the problem.

  On the other hand, if a person's track record is one of love and grace, and what others are accusing them of seems out of character with what you've observed over the long haul, then it's probably not true and they're in the right.

- *Whose purpose is redemptive?* This relates to a person's motive, which you can observe by carefully examining the facts. Who is trying to advance the cause of Christ and His redemptive purpose in the world? Who is trying to promote unity and peace?

- *Who is acting like a Christian?* The person who isn't acting like a Christian, probably isn't in the right. Regardless of the wrong done to a believer or the anger they may feel, they must never forget they represent Jesus. People watching believers make decisions about church, faith, and God by watching those lives. In all things . . . at all times . . . believers must act like Jesus!

The Rest of the Story

Jackson and the church resolved their conflict. Jackson left the staff, but the church decided not to sue and even offered him a generous severance. People who had been hurt and angry were involved in the peacemaking process. That church is doing wonderful things for the Kingdom, and Jackson is a successful pastor who is determined not to repeat his mistakes.

Unfortunately, Ezra and Rachael and Samuel and Beth never resolved their conflict. They now attend separate churches and do their best to avoid each other in the community. The ministry they were all part of didn't survive. People on opposite sides of the conflict still act with anger and hate. God only knows what Kingdom potential they forfeited in exchange for the momentary satisfaction of winning. I still regularly pray for peace.

Stuff to consider . . .

1. Make a list of the last several conflicts you've had, whether large or small.

2. Look for patterns in those conflicts. Does the same type of issues crop up often?

3. What lesson can you learn to avoid future conflicts?

4. For added insight, discuss your observations with a trusted friend or mentor.

5. What lessons can your team learn by looking at your conflicts as a group rather than in isolation?

5

Your Ability Won't Get You Far If People Don't Like You

I have a friend who went to a church as their new lead pastor. His preaching was great, attendance was up, income was up—but it didn't go well at all. The people didn't like him!

When he accepted the position of lead pastor at another church, he was more strategic. Before he went, we sat down together and planned his first ninety days. Every day for three months, he spent relational time with a different key leader in the church. His preaching was still great, the income was up, attendance was up—but this time, something was different. The people liked him! He had made relationships a priority.

Your talent, your intellect, and your ability won't get you far if people don't like you. In ministry, business, or even in your family, if people don't like you, they won't follow you. They might obey you, but only to keep their job, get what they want, or get you off their back. Leadership is about relationships.

I have a friend who leads a ministry in a large church. He's an excellent communicator with some wonderful gifts. But despite his many abilities, he can't build his ministry. Why? He doesn't want to spend time building relationships. He considers himself too important for that. The people might like him if he gave them a chance, but in the absence of relationship they look for another leader to follow.

Another friend is in student ministry. Honestly, he doesn't have great gifts and abilities. He's not a good communicator. In fact, when he speaks he's kind of boring. But his group and his influence continue to grow because people like him.

Am I saying that you must please everyone? Absolutely not! Trying to make everyone happy is exhausting, discouraging, and—above all—impossible. Being well-liked means that you actively cultivate healthy relationships with others. People may not like everything you do, but if they like you, they'll work with you.

If you don't like yourself, it affects every relationship in your life and every leadership opportunity.

A promotion at work likely hinges on people skills more than on production. If you want your ministry, Sunday School class, or section in choir to grow, the key is relationships. If you want to sell more cars, gain new customers, or build a network, you must develop and maintain intentional relationships. People must like you!

What it is that keeps some people from being effective in relationships? Why is it they struggle to be liked? Why are other less talented people so skilled at liking and being liked by others?

I don't want to oversimplify what can be a complex issue, but often the reason some people have trouble developing relationships is because they are insecure. They aren't confident in themselves. Because they lack confidence in themselves, they aren't effective at relating to and leading others.

If I don't like me, it's difficult for you to like me, or for me to like you. If you don't like yourself, it affects every relationship in your life and every leadership opportunity.

Stan Toler wrote an excellent book on relationships titled *The Secret Blend*. It's a quick, easy read with some wonderful principles. This is what he wrote about insecurity:

> **Truly selfish people are those who don't like themselves. They usually act out their self-loathing by putting others down, always wanting their own way, and then, when they don't get it, taking out their anger on others. Those who are at peace with themselves seldom think of self. They have that area of their lives under control, and that gives them the freedom to develop relationships with others. Jesus Christ, the wisest man who ever lived, told us to love our neighbors as we love ourselves. You see, in order to have strong outward relationships, we must have a strong inward relationship. That's why it's important for you to be on friendly terms with yourself before you start building friendships with others.[1]**

Perhaps you struggle with insecurity. I've been there. As a kid, I was painfully shy. I had hair that wouldn't stay in place, wore thick glasses, and read a book a day. That's an instant recipe for being picked on in school! The thought of giving a book report in class literally made me sick. The idea of speaking in front of a group of my peers petrified me. I was picked on and bullied.

---

1. Stan Toler, *The Secret Blend* (Colorado Springs: Waterbrook Press, 2004), 70.

In junior high, I overcompensated. I learned how to pick on and make fun of others. I was quick-witted and quick to insult. I put down others in a failed attempt to feel better about myself.

As an adult, I constantly measured myself against others. I was super competitive and cared way too much about numbers. In my eyes, more people in our church and more money in the offerings meant I was a success. But no matter what level of success I achieved, it was never enough to make me feel secure.

Thankfully, we serve a gracious God who helped me learn to see myself through His eyes and evaluate myself according to a healthy grid. My first book, *3 Questions*, was born out of that process. Today, I'm a better leader, more at peace with myself, and far less concerned about achieving success in the world's eyes. As someone who has struggled with insecurity my entire life, I want to offer help if you struggle with this issue. I'm not writing as an expert or a psychologist but as a fellow struggler.

The Differences between Secure and Insecure Leaders

Perhaps you don't struggle with insecurity, but you work for or with someone who is insecure. If you learn how to recognize when they're leading or acting out of insecurity, this will help you help them. You'll be able to live or work with them with greater understanding.

When a person leads out of insecurity, they create insecurity in others.

- Insecure parents raise insecure children.
- Insecure teachers produce insecure students.

- Insecure pastors create insecure members.
- Insecure coaches produce insecure athletes.
- Insecure managers produce insecure employees.

How do you spot an insecure leader? What are the differences between a secure leader and insecure leader? As you read this chapter, use the thoughts to evaluate yourself. They can also help you understand the leader you serve. You can even use these ideas to evaluate leaders from a distance. Whether a football coach, a pastor, a teacher, a CEO, a world leader, or a school principal, you can observe the results of their leadership and determine whether they are a secure or insecure leader.

An insecure leader takes the credit.

When someone else succeeds, an insecure leader diverts attention to their own success or input. It sounds something like this:

Employee: "I talked to John Foster. He's going to buy ten units."

Manager: "Oh, I know. I told him you could help him."

or

CEO: "Randy really did a terrific job on that project."

Manager: "Well, I gave him the idea. He never could have done it without me."

Insecure leaders make sure people know the success couldn't have happened without them. They're quick to let everyone know their contribution to the win.

A secure leader shares the credit with others.

Even if the credit for success rightfully belongs to a secure leader, they give it to others. Why? The secure leader understands it's not about who gets the credit, it's about accomplishing the mission. A secure leader wants to build up the team, and nothing builds a team quite like a shared victory. Don't keep victories to yourself! Share the credit!

Insecure leaders surround themselves with weak people.

To ensure they're admired and adored, insecure leaders make sure no one in their inner circle is as strong or stronger than they are.

I listen to pastors who complain they can't find good staff members, but in some cases they really don't want a strong team. They prefer to surround themselves with weak people because they fear the strengths of strong people might reveal their weaknesses.

Secure leaders surround themselves with strong people.

Secure leaders are comfortable with the strengths of others and will often hire staff who are strong in their areas of weakness. Their mindset is: "The stronger my team, the stronger I become. Their strengths lift me! Together we do more."

When an insecure leader evaluates themselves, they only see weaknesses.

Insecure leaders focus on everything they aren't, everything they should be, and everything they wish they were or could've been. Most of the time, they don't do this publicly, but if you listen carefully, you can pick it up in their self-talk.

This kind of leader is prone to depression, burnout, and moodiness because they're evaluating themselves against a standard they can never meet. If you dwell only on your weaknesses, you'll give up easily and resist the risks you need to take to succeed.

A secure leader acknowledges personal weaknesses and strengths.

It's interesting, but the more secure the leader, the more comfortable they are admitting their own weaknesses and what they don't do well. At the same time, what separates them from insecure leaders is that though they are transparent about their own weakness, they don't dwell on them.

One of my strengths is communicating, but I'm quite possibly the worst joke teller in the world! When I tell a joke, no one laughs. In fact, my jokes are met with painful silence. Once a year, our team talks me into trying again. I tell the joke and the crowd is silent, followed by loud laughter from the team—not laughing at the joke, but laughing at how pathetic my attempt to tell it was. I admit it. I can't tell jokes.

> A secure leader wants to build up the team, and nothing builds a team quite like a shared victory.

I love to watch other speakers like my son Parker who can captivate a room with a sense of humor. It's truly a gift—one that I don't have. I could allow that weakness of mine to become a focus and berate myself about it, but God also gave me some wonderful strengths. I'm comfortable being vulnerable in front of a crowd. I can share my passion in a way that rallies people around a cause. I'm good at writing sermons. Rather than focus on my weaknesses, I recognize that my goal as a leader is to leverage my strengths and get some strong people around me to compensate for my weaknesses. Believe me, I'm truly thankful for the great joke-tellers on our team!

An insecure leader evaluates themselves based on comparison.

Their question is "What am I doing compared to other people around me?" When you compare yourself with others you put your position, your accomplishments, your talents, your relationships, your possessions, your strengths, and your weaknesses on one side of the scale and measure them against those of someone else to determine your value or worth. The comparison method often focuses on the past. It's about making comparisons with the people they went to high school or college with, or the people who started at the same time in the company. "Look what they've done, and I haven't. If only I could be like them."

A secure leader evaluates themselves based on their potential.

Secure leaders ask questions like:

- How am I doing right now?
- Am I growing?
- Am I reaching my potential?
- Am I maximizing my strengths?

Secure leaders learn from the past but push toward the future. Don't spend your time competing against someone who isn't competing against you. That's exhausting! Instead, spend your energy moving forward!

An insecure leader can't laugh at themselves.

Insecure leaders think a mistake is a tragedy, a reason to be depressed, and a reaffirmation of their weaknesses. They respond to mistakes with negative self-talk: "I'm such a loser. I'm a failure. I messed up again. Nothing I do ever works."

A secure leader laughs at their mistakes.

Secure leaders see a mistake as another opportunity to learn. In fact, they tell stories about their mistakes as examples to others.

A few years ago, I got my license plate sticker in the mail. My car was parked right by my office so I went outside to put the sticker on the license plate.

Secure leaders learn from the past but push toward the future.

Usually, someone does that type of thing for me because I'm basically inept and clueless. I'm so mechanically challenged, I can't even put a sticker on right.

This time, I decided to do it on my own, but I couldn't figure it out. I looked everywhere and could not figure out where a "60" sticker would go. I had no idea what that "60" stood for. I knelt on the ground by my car and started thinking. At that moment, one of our students, Alex Johnson, walked by. She asked what I was doing, and I replied, "I'm trying to figure out where this '60' goes." Alex didn't say a word. She just took the sticker out of my hand and turned it over, so it read "09." How could I not laugh at myself?

An insecure leader resists evaluation.

The insecure leader often evaluates others harshly, but is unwilling to be evaluated themselves. It hurts too much to hear about areas that need improving. An insecure leader is uncomfortable asking questions like these:

- What could I have done better?
- How can I improve next time?
- Did I do anything that made you cringe?
- How could I have maximized the moment?
- Can I do anything to make it a greater success?

They won't ask the question, because the answer hurts too much. They've fallen for a classic lie: "My performance equals my self-worth."

A secure leader embraces evaluation and input from others as an opportunity to grow.

In fact, a secure leader creates forums to get that input. They ask for evaluation!

Every Monday morning, a creative team evaluates my weekend message. They go over what I did well, what worked, and what didn't work. Over time I've learned to be the first to offer an evaluation. Before anyone speaks, I talk about what I think I did well and where I failed. I do that to create an atmosphere that releases people to evaluate me. I don't want anyone to hold back their input just because I'm the leader.

To be clear—unsolicited, random input is rarely helpful. But strategic, targeted, requested input from wise people is almost always helpful.

An insecure leader produces followers.

Insecure leaders don't raise up leaders because they're afraid those leaders might expose their weaknesses. They may have loyal followers, but very few leaders. Any secure leaders who somehow make it on the team won't stay long! There's no room for them. With an insecure leader, it's most often a one-person show.

> You can tell the quality of a leader by the quality of the people who work for them.

A secure leader produces leaders.

You can tell the quality of a leader by the quality of the people who work for them. A good team won't keep working for an insecure leader.

Pastors often ask me why they can't seem to get good staff. The truth is, you don't get good staff; you develop good people into good staff. You recruit individuals who have the willingness and potential to learn, and you teach them to be strong leaders. They may not be impressive at the start but when a secure leader molds and shapes them, they grow into an amazing team.

A strong leader attracts secure leaders to the organization. The more secure the leader, the more secure people want to work with them.

An insecure leader only experiences success for a season.

An insecure leader can experience success, just not lasting success. An insecure leader doesn't build an organization that can stand the test of time because, as the star of the show, the majority of the power, decision-making, and control is centered on them. The organization cannot grow beyond the ability of the insecure leader to control it.

A secure leader enjoys enduring success.

A secure leader continually thinks about what's next. They ask questions like these:

What will happen after I'm gone?

How can I ensure we keep growing?

What people can I bring around me to take us to the next level?

An insecure leader keeps the blessings to themselves.

The perks, the pay, the key relationships, and exciting opportunities all belong to the insecure leader, because they are the leader.

A secure leader shares the blessings!

Secure leaders want their team to be well-compensated and appreciated. They willingly share relationships, opportunities, and blessings.

In my second year as pastor, John Maxwell asked me a question: "Rod, if you found a staff member who could take your church to the next level, but you had to pay them a higher salary than your own, would you still hire them?"

It took me a moment to answer. It challenged my ego. I'm the leader. I should rightfully make the most money. But after thinking about it, my answer was yes. Doing what's best for the church matters more to me than receiving the highest salary. John's question became reality. I've had staff members with a higher salary than mine. I don't resent that; I celebrate that!

An insecure leader produces insecure followers.

One of my friends worked for a leader whose basic leadership philosophy was to keep the people around him off-balance. He didn't want anyone to get too comfortable. He would actually say that to the team! The result was an insecure, weak, underperforming team. But this let the leader be the star.

A secure leader produces secure leaders.

If you see an organization filled with secure leaders, that didn't happen by accident. That's the product of a secure leader building an effective team. Secure leaders are comfortable with the successes of others and they want the people around them to operate in their strengths.

How to Become a Secure Leader

Which type of leader are you—secure or insecure? As you read through this chapter, did you identify more with the attributes of a secure leader or an insecure leader? Perhaps you didn't need to read the material to discover what type of leader you are. You already knew!

If, like me, you struggle with insecurity, you don't have to stay that way! You can grow, change, and learn to become a secure leader. This is by no means an exhaustive list but let me give you some ways to begin to change.

Learn how God views you.

Insecurity comes when you see yourself through your eyes instead of God's. Get a true picture of yourself through His eyes. Post this list of affirmations and Scriptures where you can see them every day. Replace your negative thoughts about yourself with God's amazing thoughts about you!

- *God wants to use you.*

If you keep yourself pure, you will be a special utensil for honorable use. Your life will be clean, and you will be ready for the Master to use you for every good work. (2 Timothy 2:21, NLT)

- *You are righteous.*

We are therefore Christ's ambassadors, as though God were making his appeal through us. We implore you on Christ's behalf: Be reconciled to God. God made him who had no sin to be sin for us, so that in him we might become the righteousness of God. (2 Corinthians 5:20–21)

- *You are special.*

But you are not like that, for you have been chosen by God himself—you are priests of the King, you are holy and pure, you are God's very own—all this so that you may show to others how God called you out of the darkness into his wonderful light. Once you were less than nothing; now you are God's own. Once you knew very little of God's kindness; now your very lives have been changed by it. (1 Peter 2:9–10, TLB)

- *God has a plan for you.*

"For I know the plans I have for you," declares the Lord, "plans to prosper you and not to harm you, plans to give you hope and a future." (Jeremiah 29:11)

- *You are God's friend.*

This includes you who were once so far away from God. You were his enemies and hated him and were separated from him by your evil thoughts and actions, yet now he has brought you back as his friends ... Christ has brought you into the very presence of God, and you are standing there before him with nothing left against you. (Colossians 1:21–22, TLB)

- *You are chosen.*

It is he who saved us and chose us for his holy work not because we deserved it but because that was his plan long before the world began—to show his love and kindness to us through Christ. (2 Timothy 1:9, TLB)

• *You can do what God calls you to do.*

I can do everything God asks me to with the help of Christ who gives me the strength and power. (Philippians 4:13, TLB)

Spend time with secure leaders and friends.

It's odd, but you almost always find insecure people grouped together. Insecure people tend to congregate with other insecure people. That's the opposite of what you need to do. It may go against your natural tendencies at first but spending time with secure people will ultimately make you feel more secure. Secure leaders don't compete with you. They don't push you down to build themselves up. They don't respond to your victories by sharing their bigger victories. They celebrate with you. They want to see you succeed, advance, and grow. Paul demonstrated an understanding of this principle when he instructed us to "equip [God's] people for works of service so that the body of Christ may be built up" (Ephesians 4:12). God's clear intent for us is to encourage and strengthen one another, not tear each other down.

Not only does this align with biblical principles of loving your neighbor, it also makes sense in a more practical way because, "As each part does its own special work, it helps the other parts grow, so that the whole body is healthy and growing and full of love" (Ephesians 4:16, NLT). As you spend time with leaders and friends who are settled enough in their own sense of self to work and live alongside you without competition or comparison, you'll feel energized and empowered to do the same.

Recognize when your reactions are based on insecurity.

If your reactions to people or situations are based on inse-curity, learn to recognize that and practice positive self-talk. Tell yourself the truth! No book, program, or seminar will help you build lasting security; in fact, Paul said, "If you think you are standing strong, be careful not to fall" (1 Corinthians 10:12, NLT). Read Scriptures that tell you how God sees you. Allow what He says about you to inform your opinion of yourself.

Spend more time with God.

The Lord is loving, affirming, restorative, and kind. As Jude instructed, "But you, dear friends, must build up your lives ever more strongly upon the foundation of our holy faith, learning to pray in the power and strength of the Holy Spirit. Stay always within the boundaries where God's love can reach and bless you. Wait patiently for the eternal life that our Lord Jesus Christ in his mercy is going to give you" (Jude 20–21, TLB) There's a wonderful peace that comes in His presence. The more time you spend pray-ing, reading your Bible, and worshipping, the more secure you'll feel. As you immerse yourself in His presence, you'll experience what Jude described as "the eternal life" (Jude 21, TLB).

Embrace God's plan for your life.

Not your plan. Not your parent's plan. Make it your aim to please God. His plan is the best one for your life. Receive the truth that "He has created us anew in Christ Jesus, so we can do the good things he planned for us long ago" (Ephesians 2:10, NLT). God has designed work especially for you. Embrace His plan and follow it with everything you have!

Remember that His plan for your life is different than His plan for my life or Joel Osteen's life. When you try to follow the plan for someone else's life, you'll undoubtedly become insecure. When David went to fight Goliath, Saul tried to convince David to wear his armor into battle, but David shook it off. It wasn't made for him. He knew it would ultimately become an obstacle. Don't embrace God's plan for someone else's life. You'll never be able to achieve it, and it'll become an obstacle that causes great insecurity. It wasn't made for you! Instead, embrace God's plan for your life.

Your church may never be as big as Lakewood Church. Your business may never be as big as Walmart. You may never have as much money as Warren Buffett. But, you can embrace and accomplish God's plan for your life.

Instead of comparing your life to someone else's life or achievements, think this way: *This is what God created me for. This is what He designed me to do. Nothing else could make me more fulfilled. I may not be the most well-known, I may not lead the biggest business, I may not make the most money, but with my whole heart, I will follow His plan. I will do what He created me to do!*

Paul's wholehearted embrace of God's plan for his life is a good model for us to follow. He told the Philippian believers, "I trust that my life will bring honor to Christ, whether I live or die. For to me, living means living for Christ, and dying is even better" (Philippians 1:20–21, NLT). Whether living or dying, Paul was determined to complete the work God had called him to do.

God has a good plan for you, too!

Stuff to consider . . .

1. Make a list of your worst or funniest mistakes, then practice laughing at yourself.

2. Experiment with having someone evaluate something you presented. Ask them to evaluate your strengths and weaknesses.

3. Make a list of the way you tend to see yourself and compare it with the way God sees you.

4. Describe why God's plan for your life is the best plan.

6

A Leader Leads Everybody, Not Just a Select Group

One of the biggest challenges in leadership is working with diverse types of people. In the organization, business, ministry, or department you lead, you most likely deal with a wide variety of personalities—and you probably have them all in the same meeting! As the leader, you must figure out how to work with all these personalities, to help them not only advance the cause of the organization, but grow and become who God intends for them to be. How secure or insecure a person is in their position will have a dramatic effect on the way you lead them, and everyone falls in a different place along the spectrum. You may even discover that a person who seems very secure in one area is racked by insecurity in another. Identifying people's insecurities is key to leading them, as both ends of the spectrum present different and unique tests.

As a leader, you probably struggle to know how to work with insecure people—what to say and do to help them be the best God created them to be. You see the potential, you know what they can be, but they lack self-confidence. Working with insecure people can take a lot of time, and an equal amount of patience. But if you can help an insecure person become confident, they'll be intensely loyal to you.

I entered "insecurity" on Google and got over thirty-seven million results! Someone who is insecure lacks confidence in themselves. Typically they're afraid to try new things or meet new people. Insecurity also leads to attention-seeking behavior, especially seeking approval. The insecure person then clings to anyone who gives them that approval. Someone who is insecure is easier to manipulate and more likely to follow whichever crowd gives them acceptance. Insecure people doubt their value and struggle with feelings of worthlessness.

Effectively working with an insecure person is especially difficult if you, too, are insecure. After all, you can't effectively instill confidence in others if you don't have confidence in yourself. Your own lack of confidence won't allow you to give confidence to someone else, or they become a threat. It's difficult for insecure people to make other people feel secure.

There are a lot of books about self-esteem and building self-confidence, but there are few resources that teach you how to work with someone who is insecure and help them become confident. As you read in the previous chapter, I have firsthand experience at being insecure! As a result, I'm drawn to people who are like I was: desperately needing acceptance and approval, and searching for validation. I'd like to share some principles I've learned that will help you bring out the best in insecure people.

How to Bring Out the Best in Insecure People

Find something in which the insecure person can succeed.

Nothing creates confidence like success. Everyone needs to be good at something. The area of success matters far less than the success itself. Find any area!

When Greg Robins first came to our church, he was the most insecure, introverted person I'd ever met. He wouldn't look you in the eye, speak to you, or visibly respond if you spoke to him. Yet he kept coming to church. Our team decided we needed to find a place where Greg could serve and succeed. We threw out idea after idea, but nothing seemed to fit. Finally, Pam Harrell, our director of Membership Services, had an idea. Greg would become the leader of an all-new ministry: the thermostat ministry. We have more than thirty heating and cooling units on our campus. Early every Sunday morning, Greg walked through the entire complex, setting each thermostat to a comfortable temperature. If there was a problem with a unit, Greg left a note for our building supervisor. After a year leading the thermostat ministry (he was the only member!), Greg grew to the place where he would speak to members of our team. Greg's first success was small and may have seemed insignificant, but it was the first time he had successfully led something. He felt valued!

Eventually, we approached Greg with the idea for another ministry. We asked him to lead the staff shuttle ministry. Our staff arrives very early on Sunday morning and parks about half a mile from the building. Every week Greg arrived before 6:00 a.m. and drove a shuttle bus back and forth from the staff parking area to the front door of the church. He never grew to the point where he would initiate a conversation, but after a few months, when we greeted him, he would respond.

I'll never forget Greg's first Christmas in the staff shuttle ministry. The whole team came up with a plan. We assigned arrival times to each staff member—three to five minutes apart—so everyone would have one-on-one time with Greg in the shuttle.

We all brought him a wrapped Christmas gift, and when we got on the shuttle, each person told him, "Merry Christmas, Greg. I love and appreciate you. Your ministry matters."

By the end of the morning, Greg had a pile of unopened gifts next to him at the front of the bus. He asked the last staff member, "What do I do? I've never received a Christmas present before." Greg didn't know what to say or what to do with his wrapped gifts.

Greg became a trusted friend and valuable volunteer. It all started with the thermostat ministry—a ministry we created specifically so he could succeed. Develop opportunities for the more insecure members of your team to succeed. Success generates its own inertia, but some people need a little help getting started.

Celebrate small successes.

After you've found a place for the person to succeed, celebrate that success! Don't be fake or over-the-top with your celebration but find a creative way to recognize and affirm the person.

When dealing with an insecure person, it's important to celebrate before you evaluate. If you evaluate first, they'll be so focused on the negative feedback, they won't hear or remember the celebration.

Gently affirm.

When I was in third grade, my family moved to another city. I really struggled to fit in at my new school, with new kids. I was miserable. I cried every day when it was time to go to school. My parents had a conference with my teacher, Mrs. Olson, and told her how I was feeling. Mrs. Olson decided to make me her personal project, but she did it in a way that backfired. She singled me out for attention in front of the class. Several times a day, she asked how I was doing. It was obvious to everyone in the class that Mrs. Olson was trying to help me. That made my situation even worse! I got more negative attention as other kids made fun of me for being the teacher's pet.

To the insecure person, over-the-top or forced affirmation comes across as fake. They can quickly spot a made-up compliment. Mrs. Olson wanted to help me, but she made things worse. I knew she wasn't being sincere.

The summer after my ninth-grade year, my family moved to Irving, Texas, and started attending Calvary Temple. My youth pastor was Darius Johnston. Somehow, Darius saw something in me that I didn't see in myself. He decided to give attention and affirmation to a shy, awkward teenager and did it in a skillful, gentle way. Darius spent time with me without pressure. He seemed to enjoy being with me! Darius also included me in

When dealing with an insecure person, it's important to celebrate before you evaluate.

his circle. When people went out to eat with him, I was there. His visible approval led others to accept me. Darius wrote thank-you notes to me, ate dinner with me and my family, and trusted me with responsibility. Slowly, Darius helped me develop confidence in myself and in God's call on my life.

One of the things I regularly get criticized for is that I always seem to have a "project": someone who is insecure and maybe even a little bit needy who I am working with. I've been told things like, "You need to spend more time with leaders. You need to spend time with influential people and high-capacity leaders where you can get the greatest possible return." Perhaps those critics mean well (I'm not really sure), but they don't understand. I was once a "project." Now, I get to give what I received. I'm determined to be a gentle affirmer for others, the way Darius was with me.

When I look across our congregation, I see my former projects. Some of them now serve on our staff! It brings me tremendous joy to see them leading people and making a difference.

> **The highest form of affirmation focuses on validating the person, not their performance.**

Gentle affirmers are a rare and wonderful blessing. With gentle affirmation, there's no sense of competition, positioning, or an agenda. These people are quiet with their affirmation and don't push you to change quickly. Gentle affirmers are patient with God's process in your life. They recognize that insecurity is an intensely personal and private pain. They don't "go public" with their affirmation and are never over-the-top with fake praise. Gentle affirmers understand the next key to working with insecure people.

When you affirm an insecure person, don't just focus on what they do but affirm who they are.

Affirm the insecure person's character more than you affirm their conduct or performance. When you affirm the performance of an insecure person, you reinforce their insecurity. They think, *Oh, no! Now I must do that just as well next time.* Or, *They only care about me because of what I do.*

If you've never felt insecure, it's difficult for you to understand this principle. You may even think I'm being unreasonable. But the highest form of affirmation focuses on validating the person, not their performance. To effectively affirm, say things like this:

- I really enjoy spending time with you.
- It makes me smile when I see you.
- I love you.
- I thank God for you.
- I believe in you.
- I'm glad you work with me.
- I wouldn't want to do this without you.
- You add real value to the church and to me.
- I'm proud of you.

When you say, "I am proud of you," the insecure person may ask, "Why are you proud of me?" How you respond is key. Don't let your answer be about something that person did. Instead, affirm who they are.

Carter was an incredibly insecure student. I recognized it and decided to become the chief gentle affirmer in his life. One day, Carter asked, "Why are you proud of me?" I knew my response was crucial. I said, "I watch people. I've noticed how you treat everyone the same—with gentle love and encouragement. You make people feel good. In fact, you make me feel good. I always enjoy spending time with you." That conversation was a key moment in Carter's life. He discovered that his pastor enjoyed spending time with him. I was able to be for Carter what Darius was for me when I was the same age. I pray one day Carter will be that gentle affirmer for someone else!

Does that mean you can never praise an insecure person for their performance? Of course not. There are moments when you can—and should—praise their performance. The key is, don't just talk about performance; always include personal affirmation as well. Say things like: "You're always so helpful. Thank you for rearranging the chairs in my office." The insecure person sees nonspecific performance praise as fake, even manipulative. Be specific in your performance praise and general in your personal praise.

Document your praise.

Don't just give verbal affirmation. When you write a note, the person will keep it forever and read it again at moments of insecurity.

Your documented praise lives forever. Years ago, when I taught junior high Sunday School, we did an affirmation exercise at the end of a lesson. I taped a piece of paper on everyone's back and handed out pens. We spent twenty minutes writing compliments and affirmations on each other's backs.

That exercise isn't original to me. I'm sure others have found a way to do it even more creatively and effectively. But ten years later, when I was in the home of one of those students, she opened her closet door and on the back of her door I saw the sheet of paper from that day in Sunday School. She still looked at those words of affirmation every single morning.

A few years ago, our team did a similar exercise. We each wrote ten thank-you notes every week for an entire year and gave them to people in our church. What amazing comments we received! We actually received thank-you cards for our thank-you notes!

I have a "good letter" file. When I get a note of encouragement or a kind card, I drop it in the file. When I'm having a difficult day or feeling a little down, I randomly pull a card from the file and read it. This always brightens my day! Don't just speak praise and affirmation; write it down. Let it live forever.

Teach insecure people how to disagree properly.

Insecure people don't usually know how to disagree well with others. Because they take things so personally, insecure people tend to present things personally, with too much emotion. They need to learn to remove emotion from disagreement and to understand that evaluating the situation doesn't have to devalue the person who did it.

> **Don't just speak praise and affirmation; write it down. Let it live forever.**

A crash course in proper disagreement is good for all of us. Make sure that everyone on your team understands these concepts:

- *Proper disagreement is said at the right time.* It isn't said in the heat of the moment or when people are in a hurry, but when the pressure is off or the event is over.
- *Proper disagreement is said in the right place.* If your disagreement is with one person, it needs to be said to that person, rather than in a public setting. Public meetings are rarely the appropriate place to process disagreements.
- *Proper disagreement is said in the right way.* If you have emotions or ego tied up in the issue, save it for another day.

Wait until you can say it in a calm, reasonable way. Often, effective disagreement is lost because someone sounds angry and defensive. Remember: If the other person *thinks* you're mad, you might as well be mad!

- *Proper disagreement is said with the right goal.* The aim should be to fix a problem, heal a hurt, or unite a group. In proper disagreement, the goal is to make everyone better. Strengthening or preserving the relationship is a central priority.

- *Proper disagreement isn't criticism.* Criticism has a different goal: to tear down. Disagreement is said to you. Criticism is said to someone else. We should encourage disagreement and discourage criticism. Criticism is, "I know better what you should have done." Disagreement is, "Can we work this out and be better together?"

- *Proper disagreement doesn't have a winning side.* No one wins a disagreement. Instead, everyone works together to reach a solution.

Secondhand affirmation powerfully affirms the insecure.

Instead of merely speaking affirmation to the insecure person, share it with someone close to them like their spouse or parents. When the insecure person hears your affirmation through others, they don't suspect a hidden agenda or motive for your kind words and they'll be more likely to believe what you said.

Some may say secondhand praise is manipulative because it's given with false pretense; after all, the message is intended less for the hearer than for the person it's about. While I understand the argument, the difference is that secondhand affirmation is intended to build someone up, not bend them to your will. In addition, it's a subtle way of offering public praise to a person who might otherwise be resentful of such attention.

Secondhand affirmation is also the most powerful form of praise. I utilize it often. Last week, I told Margie, "Your husband did a remarkable job leading in worship this morning. I so appreciate his sensitivity to the Spirit and to others." As soon as Margie got home, she told Matt what I had said. He sent me this text: "Thank you for what you said to my wife. That really made me feel good about myself. Means a lot to me. I love you."

> **Secondhand affirmation is also the most powerful form of praise.**

A member of our staff who works in student ministry makes a habit of sending post cards to students when she senses they or their families could use some extra encouragement. Not only does the student read it, but the parents get to see what another trusted adult thinks of their child, without invading the student's privacy. It's an effective way to affirm the student and the parents at the same time.

When insecure people make a mistake, quickly affirm your commitment.

The first time someone makes a mistake, they fear how you'll react. This can be a key moment in the relationship. Don't let a moment of uncontrolled anger or emotion undo all the hard work you've done.

In your ministry, organization, or family, create a culture where it's okay to make mistakes, and where people respond to failures with love, forgiveness, and grace. People find security in an environment where they are loved and valued, even when they make a mistake. It's an environment where "love covers over all wrongs" (Proverbs 10:12) and the person who "covers over an offense" promotes love (Proverbs 17:9). *Anyone* who has made a mistake can recover in that kind of environment!

Let insecure people see you helping others feel secure and ask them to assist you!

It's powerful when an insecure person begins to help build security in another insecure person. As they affirm and encourage someone else, it builds their confidence.

Your goal as a leader should be to help people develop not only self-confidence but the "God-confidence" that comes when they realize they're an important part of His body. In 1 Corinthians 12, Paul wrote that, like the individual organs of the human body, we each have our own identities; however, when we choose to follow Christ, we become part of a greater purpose, an "integrated life in which [Jesus] has the final say in everything" (1 Corinthians 12:13, MSG). We become the body of Christ. Once we are members of His body, our individual significance is not diminished but strengthened since it takes "all the different-but-similar parts arranged and functioning together" (v. 15) for the body to perform optimally. At the same time, being part of the body of Christ also "keeps your significance from getting blown up into self-importance. For no matter how significant you are, it is only because of what you are a part of" (v. 19) that you are significant.

One of the great strengths of the body of Christ is that "every part [is] dependent on every other part" (v. 25). It is within His body that we all find our true significance, and helping an insecure person find their place is the most fulfilling project of all. As Paul concluded, "You are Christ's body—that's who you are! You must never forget this. Only as you accept your part of that body does your 'part' mean anything" (vv. 27–28). Connect the insecure members of your team to the body of Christ and watch them flourish.

How to Bring Out the Best in Secure People

On the other end of the spectrum, and equally challenging for many leaders, is working with a secure person, especially if that person is more secure than the leader! Just as you can learn how to lead and love insecure people, so you can learn to lead and love people who are secure. First, let's blow up some common myths:

Loud = Secure

Not true. In fact, most often the opposite is true. Loud, opinionated people often are trying to hide their insecurity with volume. Some of the most insecure people I know are loud and boisterous, while some of the most secure people I know are quiet.

Controlling = Secure

Again, not true. Controlling people are afraid of or uncomfortable with anyone or anything that isn't under their direct control. They try to exert that control over you because they're afraid of how the relationship will be defined if they're not in control.

Popular = Secure

Some of the most popular kids in school are the most insecure kids. Part of the reason is that popularity holds you hostage. If your security is based on your popularity, what happens if you suddenly become unpopular? You don't know what to do. As a result, you do whatever you have to do to remain popular.

When you see someone who's popular and accepted, you assume they're secure. You assume that the guy who makes everyone laugh is confident and secure. But often, insecure people hide behind their funny-person role. I was an expert at that in junior high. I could make you laugh forever. But the humor was a clever way to hide my insecurity and avoid revealing my true feelings. I learned you can be the life of the party, but still feel incredibly alone.

> **A secure person is comfortable with who God made them to be.**

Successful = Secure

Some of the most successful people I know are insecure. Security isn't about what you have, it's about who you are. Possessions don't make you feel secure. In fact, they can have the opposite effect. If your self-worth is connected to your possessions, you fear the results of losing those possessions.

Position = Secure

You look at somebody who's attained a position and think, *They must be really secure.* But some people in high positions are incredibly insecure. In some cases, that's why they seek those positions. The position serves to validate their worth.

Have you ever wondered why a title matters so much to someone at work? Every time they get a new title, they print new business cards and new door plates, and makes sure everyone knows their new position. They're demonstrating their insecurity. The title helps them feel important, which in turn, makes them feel good about themselves.

Intelligent = Secure

Intelligence has nothing to do with security. I was one of the most intelligent kids in my school . . . and perhaps the most insecure. In fact, my intelligence made me even more insecure because it made me different. You tend to see loud, controlling, popular, intelligent, and successful people in high positions as secure because those characteristics expose your own insecurities.

Many times, when someone comes to me and wants to know how to work with a secure person, I must point out that the person in focus isn't secure at all. They're simply adept at camouflaging their insecurities. So, how do you recognize someone who is secure? What does it really mean to be secure?

A secure person is comfortable with who God made them to be. They recognize their strengths, but also acknowledge their weaknesses. *Settled* is a word that isn't used much in our culture anymore—but it accurately describes a secure person. They know their value isn't determined by performance, but by the price Jesus paid for them on the cross. Someone who's secure is confident in the knowledge that God loves them despite their failures, and that He will continue to love them. Someone who is secure is convinced that God has a purpose for their life, and they are committed to follow His plan and purpose. They focus on God's plan, not their own plan or anyone else's plan.

Someone who is secure is also humble. They aren't position-oriented but rejoice in being a servant. Some people exhibit false humility: They continually use self-deprecating humor, talk down about themselves, and apologize for letting you down and not measuring up. But the truly humble person doesn't talk bad about themselves. They don't compete with others for attention or recognition; they simply focus on doing everything they can for God.

Secure people are forward looking; they don't beat themselves up over the past. Instead, they spend their energy on growing and improving. They know they can't grow forward as long as they are looking backwards.

It can be intimidating to work with people who are more secure than you, but if you're going to accomplish wonderful things for God, you need to be able to lead highly qualified, secure, mature leaders. The biggest key to working with secure people is to be secure yourself. The problem is, that won't happen overnight! Be patient with yourself. Submit to the growth process by allowing the Lord to stretch you out of your comfort zone to lead people more secure than yourself. Over the years, I've learned some keys for working with secure people.

When working with secure people, share information earlier.

Insecure people struggle with partially developed plans. The incompleteness makes them even more insecure. They also struggle if they hear a plan and the plan completely changes. You must wait to share a plan with insecure people until it is fully developed.

In contrast, when you're working with a secure person you can share information earlier in the process. When you share information early, you honor them and involve them in the process. Secure people can handle both early and partial information. Bring them into the loop earlier than you would other people.

Instead of informing secure people of decisions, give them a chance to offer input into the decision-making process.

Secure people like to be involved in the thinking process—even if the ultimate decision is different from their own. A good principle to remember is this: If a person can't handle a different decision, they aren't secure.

Secure people enjoy the process. At a key time in the growth and development of our church, I asked a group of businessmen to join "Pastor Rod's Lunch Group." These men are all great thinkers! I met with them and laid out the challenges I was facing as a leader. I just gave them the facts and then listened. They gave input. They challenged my way of thinking and our processes.

When we were considering adding a third service (we have four now!), I met with the Lunch Group. I laid out the challenges involved in this potential change: (1) our volunteers' time commitment would increase, (2) teams would be stretched, and (3) staff would have to work harder and longer. I shared how I was wrestling with the decision and the timing.

When I finished sharing my dilemma, one of the guys looked at me and said, "Let me make sure I understand this. You can increase your capacity by a third at no cost?" I said, "What do you mean?" He said, "So you can add a third more people and it will cost you no more dollars?" I said, "Well, yeah." He looked at me and said, "You're an idiot. Why aren't you doing it already?" He then talked about capacity, flow, and multiple distribution channels. I took notes as fast as I could! He helped me think in a unique way. A few months later, we launched our third service, with almost no opposition.

When working with secure people, don't "power up" unnecessarily.

I see this often in church settings. When a pastor who is insecure has a conflict or a disagreement with a church member who is secure, the pastor looks at that person and "powers up": "I'm the pastor! I'm the leader, and we're doing it *my* way!"

Insecure leaders sometimes do that to prove they're in control, to demonstrate that they're the leader. But when you do that, you lose respect from secure people who easily recognize your need to prop yourself up on the importance of your title or position. Don't power up unless it involves a direct confrontation in front of others. In those situations, you must confront the person who challenged you, or they become the new leader. But, other than that, don't power up. I've been lead pastor for more than fifteen years. I've never had to power up.

Allow secure people to be strong in their giftedness.

Don't be intimidated when a secure person knows more than you or can do something better than you. That's why you need them!

Our chief financial officer, Miranda, is much better with accounting principles and bookkeeping than I am. So, I don't balance the checkbook at our church (or at my home!). I let Miranda operate in her strength.

I'm not good at graphics. I know nothing about creating logos, choosing fonts, or all the technical things that go into making something look good. So, when we discuss graphics in meetings, I lean on Parker, Reta, Aaron, Brian, and Tim. They're all much stronger than I in that area. It would be stupid of me to make the decision in an area where I'm weak.

Learn from the strengths of secure people.

Ask questions. Say, "I don't understand" and, "I don't know. Will you show me?" Secure people love that! They don't lose respect for you when you admit a lack of knowledge. You gain their respect for your desire to learn!

Years ago, my pastor, Alton Garrison, assigned me to lead a building project. He put me in charge of leading the process to design, bid, and build a twenty-five thousand square foot administrative complex. There was one problem: I didn't know a thing about building!

Don't be intimidated when a secure person knows more than you or can do something better than you.

The only way I could succeed was to learn from others.

When the building process started, every day the job foreman had a list of questions for me. I listened carefully, wrote them down, and then said, "Let me think about it. I'll have an answer for you first thing in the morning."

Every evening at 5:30, Jim Morris met me at the building site. Jim had served as a contractor for the Arkansas National Guard and had built many buildings. We walked around the site and I asked Jim all the questions the foreman had asked me that day. Jim not only answered the questions but carefully explained the process and principles, and made sure I understood what he was talking about.

The next morning, I met with the foreman and answered every one of his questions. I never told him about Jim. Jim wouldn't have wanted me to. At the end of the construction process, the owner of the construction company told Alton that I was the smartest customer they had ever worked with! I knew nothing about construction, but I was smart enough to learn from someone who did. A few months ago, at Jim's funeral, I finally told this story and revealed the real brains behind the building!

God has gifted you with secure people. Instead of being intimidated by their strengths, learn from them! You ascribe value to them when you allow them to teach you in the area of their strength.

Challenge their thinking.

People who are secure love to be challenged. Don't be afraid to question their logic or challenge their thought-processes. Someone who is secure not only respects that, but their loyalty to you grows. If someone gets defensive when their thinking is challenged, they aren't secure.

Give secure people room to fail.

If you give an insecure person enough room to fail, when they fail your relationship may suffer, but the secure person will quickly bounce back from the failure. You can give them a lot more freedom to make decisions because if it goes wrong, they'll own it and can handle it. In fact, secure people often thrive in an environment where they feel free to make their own decisions and navigate through the consequences. Too much of a safety net can feel stuffy to them, as if they're being micromanaged instead of led.

Give secure people affirmation and recognition.

We sometimes mistakenly think that secure people don't need affirmation and recognition. We've almost made it a spiritual gift to make sure they don't get a "big head." Everyone enjoys affirmation, and everyone is motivated by recognition. Thank them for their contributions, just like you do with anyone else.

Stay connected to the secure.

Insecure people pull on you for your time—you stay connected with them whether you want to or not. With secure people, you must be more intentional at connecting. Staying current in your relationship with them will be as much a source of encouragement to you as it is to them.

Secure people want to trust and be trusted.

Secure people want your trust, and they want to give you their trust. They're more willing to trust others than insecure people, not because they're better but because they're more confident in their discernment. They're also more confident in their ability to bounce back if you let them down.

As a follower of Jesus, what is your attitude supposed to be toward others? Celebrate the secure and their strengths and help the insecure in their weaknesses. Paul wrote about this dual capacity of leadership in Romans.

> One of the things I always pray for is the opportunity, God willing, to come at last to see you. For I long to visit you so I can bring you some spiritual gift that will help

> you grow strong in the Lord. When we get together,
> I want to encourage you in your faith, but I also want
> to be encouraged by yours (Romans 1:10–12, NLT).

Paul celebrated the strength of their faith, pointing out that their confidence in the Lord was a source of encouragement to him as well. At the same time, he demonstrated compassion to those weaker than himself as he instructed the believers: "We who are strong must be considerate of those who are sensitive about things like this. We must not just please ourselves. We should help others do what is right and build them up in the Lord" (Romans 15:1–2, NLT).

Regardless of how secure each member of your team feels, you have the responsibility not only to lead them but to give them the opportunity to function at their best. Differentiating the way you interact with them will increase their capacity to thrive.

Stuff to consider . . .

1. Which members of your team or ministry do you think are the most insecure? Take a moment to identify them and then prayerfully determine a plan to encourage them and help them find their place.

2. Write down the names of the three most secure people you know. Then, compare notes. Ask: Why are those people secure? Do you enjoy working with them, or not? Are you utilizing them in their strengths? Are you adequately affirming them for those strengths?

3. Write two thank-you notes to people who have blessed you or invested in your life. Be specific in your thanks! Then, write two more thank-you notes to people who are insecure. Consider your words carefully. Remember, people will read the notes many times.

7

Don't Go into the Pool
without a Lifeguard

For eight years, I was a volunteer employee during the summer at Wild River Country, a local water park. Somehow, I balanced my time at the water park with my role as lead pastor. My weeks were sometimes laughable. Amid writing sermons, making hospital calls, or performing weddings and funerals at the church, I made time to scoop ice cream, serve nachos, pick up trash, or vacuum pools at the water park. I know it might seem ridiculous for a pastor to do that, but my job at Wild River Country was my opportunity to work in the real world and develop intentional relationships with people who didn't know Jesus. I learned valuable lessons there and forged many friendships.

I retired in 2013 after the park sold, but for the last four years I was there, I was an unpaid, certified lifeguard. Most of the time, I worked at the wave pool. My job was straightforward: Sit with a whistle around my neck and keep people from drowning. The good news is—I was successful. The total number of drownings on my watch was zero!

The wave pool started just a few inches deep and gradually dropped to a depth of eight feet. Every ten minutes a buzzer sounded, and the waves began. That buzzer was everyone's cue to rush to the water and wade into the waves, laughing and splashing with friends. However, it was my cue to watch intently, looking for people who didn't realize the danger they were in. I watched for people who were literally in over their heads, who thought they could swim in water that deep with waves that strong.

Most people were completely confident they wouldn't fail, but from my spot on the lifeguard chair, I learned to recognize people who had overestimated their strength or skill to withstand the waves. If they went too deep, I got their attention by blowing my whistle. Then, I motioned them back to safer water.

I'll never forget one busy day at the park. The wave pool was filled with people. Instead of being on the chair, I was stationed on the side of the pool, ready to jump in or pull people out of the water. A muscular guy was trying to make it to the deep end. He was going to be "the man." I could clearly tell he wasn't. He started to struggle and then threw his hands up and shouted, "Help!" He was near the side of the pool, so I bent down from the knees, grabbed his outstretched hands, and yanked him out of the water. This big, muscular guy laid on the side of the pool deck, gasping for air.

> **If you really want to grow, you're much more likely to succeed if you establish and maintain accountability.**

After lying there for a minute, he said to me, "Can I jump back in right here?" I said, "No, sir. Not now. Not ever. You, sir, are a shallow-water-swimmer. Stay out of the deep water until you learn how to swim."

I wish I could report this was an isolated occurrence. It wasn't. Most people I fished out of the pool accepted my instructions.

Some people didn't. They didn't want someone telling them what to do, what not to do, or when to be careful. Those were the people we inevitably had to jump in and save. They ignored the whistle and the warnings. They knew better than the "dumb" lifeguard. They didn't need help. They could handle it on their own.

One of the keys to growth and positive change, and a primary mark of an effective leader, is to establish accountability: to enlist someone else to hold you responsible for your growth and change. The dictionary definition of *accountable* is "subject to the obligation to report, responsible, answerable." My definition of accountability is "answering for and giving report of your actions, words, attitudes, or behavior; owning your decisions and actions."

After you set it up, accountability software for your computer sends the person of your choice a report of every website you visit. Knowing someone is going to see that report helps you resist temptation. You're accountable to someone else for what you do online. That helps you avoid bad decisions and negative consequences.

If you're trying to lose weight, you look for an accountability partner to help you. Every week, you tell them how much weight you've gained or lost. You share your victories and your defeats. You might work out with them, or even share your food journal. On days when you're staring at a chocolate cake, the thought that you'll have to tell your accountability partner if you cave in to the craving helps you say no. Accountability helps you stick to your plan and achieve your goal.

If you struggle with lust, pornography, or sexual sin, it should be obvious that you need someone to hold you accountable, to ask the tough questions. But accountability is vital to any growth and change. If you really want to grow, you're much more likely to succeed if you establish and maintain accountability. If you won't offer and embrace accountability, you aren't likely to change.

The person who avoids accountability:

- Won't let anyone challenge their decisions or actions.
- Doesn't allow anyone to ask them tough questions.
- Takes complete, solo command of their personal growth.
- Hides weaknesses, failures, and mistakes.
- Lies about struggles.
- Refuses to answer questions, share details, or answer in any way for their actions, attitudes, or words.
- If caught doing wrong, they blame someone else.
- Never takes personal responsibility. If someone tries to make them take responsibility, they brand that person an enemy.

Doesn't that sound foolish? It's easy to see when someone else is making these mistakes, but easy to justify when you are making them.

Accountability is giving someone in your life permission to blow the whistle, to sound a warning when you are going too deep. It's asking someone to watch out for you, to help you stay safe and avoid devastating consequences. *To be accountable is to have people in your life who have the right to ask you tough questions and demand truthful answers.*

Here's a huge key. You have to offer accountability. You must decide to invite someone to be your lifeguard. Tell someone what weaknesses you're working on and give them permission to challenge you. Give them permission to ask tough questions:

- Did you take a drink?
- Did you eat healthy today?
- Did you work out?
- Did you look at pornography this week?
- Did you spend time with your family?
- Were you faithful to your wife?
- Did you lose your temper?

Choosing to be accountable isn't easy. That's why so many people avoid it. In the short run, it's easier to hide your flaws, stay away from people who challenge you, and avoid accountability. But in the long run, it's a mistake that can ruin your life.

Accountability is important because failure happens in isolation. Failure happens when you don't fear getting caught. Failure happens when you answer only to yourself. On the other hand, growth happens in community. We're safer, better, and stronger when we're together.

I've made a strategic decision to never be alone. Avoiding privacy better enables me to embrace accountability.

- Multiple members of our pastoral team have my social media and computer passwords. I encourage them to log on whenever they wish.
- My e-mail is automatically copied to a computer at home that Cindy can access.
- Virtually everyone has the passcode to unlock my phone.
- I don't travel alone. I live and work and stay in community with others.

You might be wondering: *Pastor Rod, why do you have all those safe-guards? Are you worried you'll do something wrong?* I'm not planning to fail, but I don't think anyone plans to fail. People fail because they don't put safeguards in place to prevent failure. I intentionally put people and accountability systems around me so if I'm ever tempted, I'll have lots and lots of people to blow the whistle and say, "Don't go there. Don't get in over your head. That's dangerous water." There's wonderful safety in numbers! I welcome accountability and find it in community. I don't want to be so foolish as to think it could never happen to me. I agree wholeheartedly with Paul, who wrote: "So, if you think you are standing firm, be careful that you don't fall" (1 Corinthians 10:12).

> **People fail because they don't put safeguards in place to prevent failure.**

Reasons People Avoid and Resist Accountability

If accountability is such a good thing, why do some people avoid and resist it?

They avoid accountability because it feels like control.

Some people think, *Why should I have to answer to anyone? Why should they be able to access my Internet history? They're just trying to run my life.* But that way of thinking is a trick of the Enemy. Satan doesn't want you to establish accountability. He wants you to stay alone so you're an easier target.

I've always loved to read. There was a period in middle school and high school when I read a book a day! Sometimes

I would get annoyed when my mom or dad made me stop reading so I could go to bed on time. *How dare they?* They were just trying to run my life, right? Of course not! They knew if I didn't get good rest, I would set myself up for a tough morning or maybe even struggle at school the next day. They were looking out for me, helping me make good decisions for the future when I was too focused on what was right in front of me to make them myself. That's what accountability does. Like a kid who doesn't know when to go to sleep, struggling to submit to accountability should signal your need for it. If being accountable seems like a heavy yoke, there's a good chance you're too wrapped up in your circumstances to make decisions for your own good.

They avoid accountability because it requires vulnerability.

Allowing someone to get close to you can be scary. Perhaps you've learned to avoid getting close to anyone because people close to you can hurt you. That's true. But they can also help you! If you've been hurt because of being vulnerable in the past, I'm sorry. It should never have happened. But don't give that hurt the authority to rob you of the joy of living in community with other believers now.

You are a part of the body of Christ, which "grows and builds itself up in love, as each part does its work" (Ephesians 4:16). Galatians 6:2 instructs us to "Carry each other's burdens." Be vulnerable. Allow others to carry your burdens. Your comfort zone will always be the enemy of growth.

They avoid accountability because it reveals their failures.

The very nature of accountability is you admit when you mess up, or even when you're tempted to mess up. Some people don't like that. They don't want people to know they fail. But, if you avoid accountability, people are still going to know you fail because your failure will be bigger and more devastating.

They avoid accountability because it eliminates options.

Accountability makes it difficult to continue in the questionable behavior. If you won't share your computer password or Facebook password or phone unlock code with your spouse, I'm concerned about you. It means you're keeping options open that you need to shut down. Any addict, or former addict, can tell you: If you keep your options open, you'll fail. You must get that stuff and the chance to be near that stuff completely out of your life if you ever want to be free.

They avoid accountability because they aren't firmly committed to growth and change.

When accountability stops, it stops for a reason. If I lock Cindy out of part of my life, there's a reason. You know what drives me nuts? People who say, "You don't trust me. If you really trusted me, you wouldn't ask. If you really trusted me, you wouldn't need to look." That's a manipulative cop-out and an attempt to shift blame. I respond with: "Of course, I don't trust you. I don't trust myself. That's why I'm accountable!" Submitting to accountability builds trust.

They avoid accountability because they want to continue in sin.

A person who won't accept accountability probably doesn't want to change. They don't want someone to blow the warning whistle because they don't want to stop what they're doing. It's a good sign someone is ready to change when they become totally accountable because being transparent about sin is the first step toward healing. James instructs us to "confess your sins to each other and pray for each other so that you may be healed" (James 5:16).

Submitting to accountability builds trust.

Tips for Choosing Your Accountability Partner

If you want to grow and avoid failure, offer and establish accountability with another person. As you decide who to establish as a "lifeguard" in your life, consider these things:

- Be accountable to someone ahead of you in life's journey. If they're at the same place in the journey, you may fail together.
- Be accountable to someone you respect.
- Be accountable to someone who's willing to ask tough questions and challenge you.
- Be accountable to someone you trust to keep your confidence. You should never have to worry that they'll reveal to others what you have said.
- Be accountable to someone you can be truthful with. If you lie, that's not accountability. You'll only hurt

yourself. I tell people I mentor: "I can't help you unless I know the truth. If you lie to me, I'm done. If you won't make the commitment to tell the truth, I can't help you."

- Be sure the person who holds you accountable is growing. If you're accountable to someone who's lazy, they'll only help you be lazier.

- Be accountable to someone with whom you have relationship and who is readily accessible. It would be great if everyone in our church could be accountable to me, but that's not realistic. There's no way I could possibly keep up with that many people!

Establishing accountability is one of the most important reasons to be connected to a local church. When you move from church to church, you avoid accountability because you don't have a spiritual authority in your life. You don't have to answer to anyone. You can do whatever you want. No one knows who you are, where you are, or what you're doing. There's no one to blow the whistle and warn you.

That's not God's plan for His children. He planned for us to be accountable for our actions. Believers who want to beat the system simply refuse to attach themselves to any church. God's Word provides the answer: "Two are better than one, because they have a good return for their labor: If either of them falls down, one can help the other up. But pity anyone who falls and has no one to help them up. . . . Though one may be overpowered, two can defend themselves. A cord of three strands is not quickly broken" (Ecclesiastes 4:9–12).

God designed us for community. The church is designed so you don't and won't stand alone. We're better together. "As iron sharpens iron, so one person sharpens another" (Proverbs 27:17).

Stuff to consider . . .

1. Do you have an accountability partner? Why or why not?

2. If yes, write some of the positive outcomes you've experienced from this relationship.

3. If no, write some of the reasons you have avoided developing an accountability relationship.

4. Write some ways you can overcome your hesitation to find a personal "lifeguard."

5. If you discover that your team is lacking in this discipline, decide together on some safeguards—perhaps even share passwords! As the leader, you should model accountability by offering yours first.

You Can Respond Stupidly or Wisely to Criticism and Correction

Criticism and correction are two unpleasant, but inevitable parts of any leader's journey. It's a mistake to think you're beyond either of them once you rise "high enough" in leadership. Everyone deals with critics, and everyone, at some point, needs correction. Learning to differentiate between criticism and correction, as well as how to receive and respond to them, is important in becoming an effective leader.

Criticism hurts. In this social media age, not only do you get criticized but instead of your critics sending anonymous letters written in crayon, with bad handwriting and your name misspelled, they post their angry thoughts online for the entire world to see. It's especially sad to see Christians acting this way.

Criticism keeps you from action. Critics are cruel as they hurl their opinions without thought or feeling. Their comments keep you awake at night and distract you from the mission ahead. The more public your profile, the more criticism you receive.

Before considering your response, you must first determine if what the person has said is criticism or correction. Some people talk about "constructive criticism." In my opinion, there's no such thing. I've never felt built up or "constructed" by criticism. Instead, I call helpful, evaluative comments "correction." If you misinterpret correction as criticism, you'll lose key input that's necessary for making right decisions.

Here's a grid to help you tell the difference between criticism and correction.

- Criticism is often shared with others; correction is directed to you.
- Criticism's goal is to hurt, offend, or put down; correction's goal is to fix or repair.
- Criticism is offered with an attitude of anger or pride; correction is offered in humility and love.
- Criticism attacks character; correction questions actions.
- Criticism is abusive in nature; correction is redemptive in nature.
- Criticism comes from spectators; correction comes from someone who's involved.
- The motive of criticism is to tear down or destroy; the motive of correction is to make better or refine.
- Criticism is emotional; correction is logical.
- Criticism is vague; correction is specific.
- Criticism is prone to exaggeration and lies; correction focuses on truth.

You must learn to heed the words of people who offer correction and repel destructive critics. Decide ahead of time how you'll respond!

Just before I became pastor of First Assembly, we asked the congregation to complete a survey. We discovered that only 5 percent of the people were unchurched before coming to First

Assembly. The others had come from other churches or denominational backgrounds.

As I studied those numbers, I sensed God telling us it was time for a new focus: our church needed to pivot towards reaching the unchurched. I talked to one of my mentors, John Maxwell, about the change. He told me, "Rod, before you make the change, know that if you do it, you'll lose 10 percent of the people and 10 percent of the money. Count the cost."

At our next board meeting, I shared what John had said and the inevitable criticism. I asked the board members, "If it costs us 150 people and $250,000, are you still convinced this is the right decision?" One at a time, each person answered, "I'm in."

> **You must learn to heed the words of people who offer correction and repel destructive critics.**

Then I met with our leadership team. We made a list of questions people would likely ask and developed our answers. When the questions inevitably came, we weren't caught off guard; instead, we had ready answers. Moreover, the answer was the same no matter what team member they asked. Questions aren't inherently bad, but failing to formulate responses in advance leaves you and your team coming up with answers on the fly. That kind of scramble reduces confidence among your followers and can quickly turn a person with questions into a critic.

When you're making a substantial change or changing direction, *anticipate criticism.* Put yourself in the shoes of your likely critics and list their complaints, criticisms, and questions. The goal for a leader is to *not* be surprised by criticism. Instead, expect it, anticipate it, and plan your response before you first critic speaks.

Before we ever started making the necessary changes to reach the unchurched, I began building the theological basis for change. I preached a twenty-eight-week series focused on Jesus' interactions with individuals titled "Jesus, Who Needs Him?" Over and over, I repeated a concept that—though biblical—seemed radical for our context in the Deep South: "A soul is a soul . . . is a soul . . . is a soul. Whether a black soul, white soul, fat soul, thin soul, rich soul, poor soul, every soul matters to God."

> **Even if you've anticipated the criticism and the critics, criticism still hurts.**

I also sought wisdom and guidance from our former pastor, Alton Garrison. Alton helped me shape the message and anticipate resistance. He also leveraged his influence to help people accept the change. He came as a guest speaker and celebrated the proposed changes. He even told the people that he would have made the same changes if he had still been pastor. His support and help were key to minimizing criticism.

Alton was my coach through the change. He was qualified because he had led the same church through another huge change years earlier! When Alton became pastor at First Assembly, the church had been in the same location for almost seventy-five years. Many of the people never wanted to move; however, the church's facilities were clearly inhibiting its growth. It had plateaued for more than forty years at approximately four hundred people. When Alton made the decision to move the church, he faced *lots* of criticism! I knew he was the right person to prepare me emotionally and logically for the inevitable criticism. With his help, I was able to avoid unhealthy responses that could have created unnecessary conflict. The transformation took several years, but the once-radical refrain, "Every soul matters to God," is now so deeply engrained in our church culture that it's part of our logo.

No leader should try to initiate a substantial change alone. You may not have someone with the stature, influence, and reputation of Alton to help you, but every group—no matter its size or context—has people whom others admire and respect. Enlist visible, influential supporters who will celebrate change. Do all you can to find an established leader who has faced criticism and can prepare you to face it in a healthy way—even if they operate in a different context. You'll be able to draw strength and wisdom from their experiences.

Ask yourself, "Who will my critics be? Who is most likely to resist this change?" Again, what you anticipate won't surprise you. If you know what's coming and where it's coming from, you'll be ready to respond the right way.

How to Respond Wisely to Criticism and Correction

Even if you've anticipated the criticism and the critics, criticism still hurts. Correction, even when given with the right spirit, can also be difficult to handle. Both sting! It's important that you know how to respond in a healthy way that de-escalates conflict and models proper biblical leadership. Though many people respond in unhealthy ways, you can choose differently by remembering a few principles. Interestingly, many of the same principles apply for responding to both criticism and correction.

Don't be defensive.

Don't immediately respond by defending yourself and listing all the reasons the criticism or correction is wrong. Defensive people shut down feedback loops. They no longer hear the problems. That's a dangerous place to be.

Don't deflect.

Deflection is when you respond to the criticism or correction with, "Yeah, that might be true, but did you see what Patrick did?" The goal of deflection is to refocus others away from your mistake or failure toward someone else's failing: "What I did isn't nearly as bad as what he did!" Deflection is a classic tool used by siblings. When I got in trouble as a young kid, I quickly tried to refocus my parents' attention on what my little sister did wrong. It rarely worked. In a staff situation, the leader might say, "Listen, you must schedule your events on the master calendar." The deflecting team member responds with, "Let me tell you what else we need to work on. The building isn't getting locked up properly."

Don't respond to criticism with blame.

Immature leaders are afraid of being exposed as weak, so they're quick to blame others. Strong leaders recognize their responsibility to protect and support their team at all times. The leader owns the issue.

Don't attack the person sharing the criticism.

When you attack the person offering correction or criticism, you not only devalue their comment, you devalue them. The natural response to an attack is to defend. When you attack and the other person defends, the situation escalates.

Don't respond with silence.

When you respond with silence, the other person interprets your silence through their grid. They decide whether your silence means, "You're wrong," "I don't respect you," or "I don't care what you think." Acknowledge that you have heard the person.

Don't make excuses.

When you make excuses, it invites investigation as people try to determine if your excuse is valid.

Don't be a martyr.

The martyr says, "I can't do anything right. Everyone is against me. I always mess up. I'll never overcome my past. Guess I'm just doomed to fail." Remember, even Jesus had critics! You aren't unusual because people disagree with you.

Don't go public.

It's tempting to respond to criticism by mounting a public defense. With social media, you can quickly spread your side of the story and discredit the critic. But, in doing so, you give the critic credibility and a larger platform. Once their standing is elevated by your public defense, they're more likely to escalate their criticism.

Don't chase down every critic.

The larger your platform and the greater your visibility, the more critics you'll attract. If you try to chase down and respond to every critic, you'll lose time that you could spend on the things that matter most.

For two years I logged every criticism I received. With Facebook, Twitter, and Instagram, people can broadcast their criticisms instantly. No longer is there the filter of having to write it down, find a stamp, and send an anonymous letter written in crayon with no return address. Now, people can ignore the instructions of Jesus in Matthew 18 without even hesitating!

The larger your platform and the greater your visibility, the more critics you'll attract.

Keeping track of the criticism wasn't much fun, but when I look back at the whole list it reminds me there's no way I can respond to every critic! There isn't enough space in this book to include the whole list, so I chose some of my favorites:

- You drive a BMW.
- You drive a Mercedes.
- You drive a Porsche. Actually . . . that one's true. Elton and Peggy Kirkpatrick heard me talking about always wanting a Porsche, so they bought me a remote-controlled Porsche. I drive it around my office when kids come to visit. By the way, my real vehicle is a Ford F-150 pickup.
- You fly a helicopter everywhere you go.
- You buy all your shirts at Dillard's.
- We sing too many old songs.
- We don't sing enough old songs.
- We sing too many new songs.

- We need to sing more new songs.
- You dress up too much.
- You don't dress up enough.
- Pastors shouldn't wear jeans.
- Pastors shouldn't wear pink.
- You shouldn't have a water bottle in the sanctuary. You're setting a bad example.
- You shouldn't go swimming.
- You spend too much time around students.
- You spend too much time around children.
- You spend too much time around lost people.
- You spend too much time studying.
- You don't hold up the Bible often enough when you preach.
- You use the wrong version of the Bible.
- You don't talk about politics enough.
- You talk about politics too much.
- You're a Democrat.
- You're a Republican.
- You won't tell what you are.
- You don't preach enough on the end times.
- You don't shout enough.
- You talk about money too much.
- You should talk about money more.
- You need to preach more about faith.
- You need to preach more about grace.
- You should preach more about prophecy.
- You don't talk enough about sin.
- You talk about sin too much.
- You don't talk enough about salvation.

- You preach too many salvation messages. We need "meat."
- You need to talk more about hell.
- You need to talk more about heaven.
- You need to quit talking about heaven and hell so much.
- You tell too many stories about your family.
- You should tell more personal stories.
- You should talk more about sex.
- You should never use the word *sex* in the pulpit.
- You're too skinny to be a pastor. You need to gain weight.

One of my all-time favorites was the guy who sent me an angry e-mail, absolutely incensed because I hadn't responded to his anonymous letter. Can you imagine if I tried to chase down and respond to every one of those criticisms? That would be a full-time job! Resist the impulse to defend yourself against every critic. Let your life and reputation stand for itself.

Don't overreact.

Don't abandon significant changes, alter key decisions, or change direction based on one criticism. Don't panic and assume that one loud voice represents the masses. It's more likely that voice is an isolated opinion. Don't allow critics to dictate the agenda.

Instead of quickly reacting incorrectly, wait before responding. Don't trust your first reaction! Your natural response to criticism or correction is to attack or defend. When you respond immediately, you usually regret your response.

Last week, I commented in a Facebook forum. When I read one of the replies, it made me angry. I immediately started typing my defensive response. Just before I hit "send," I decided to read the offender's post one more time. That's when I discovered I had missed one key sentence. Turns out, that person wasn't attacking me; they were defending me! It was a gentle reminder that "enthusiasm without knowledge is no good; haste makes mistakes" (Proverbs 19:2, NLT). If I hadn't taken that pause, I would've been embarrassed by my defensive and ignorant response.

Slow down. Take your time. Wait twenty-four hours. You don't have to reply to every criticism immediately.

Consider the source.

When presented with criticism or correction, ask yourself:

- Is this person loyal and faithful?
- Is this a key member of my team?
- Does this person have my best interests at heart?
- Is this person known as a critic or complainer?
- Is there a threat involved?
- Does this person claim to represent someone else?
- Could this person be right? Is there any truth in what they are saying?

Resist the impulse to defend yourself against every critic. Let your life and reputation stand for itself.

Regardless how the person presents their criticism or correction, thank them for their feedback and concern.

This isn't always easy! I often respond to criticism by saying, "Thank you for expressing your concern. I appreciate you sharing it with me first, rather than acting in an unhealthy way. I appreciate your feedback and will respond in the next forty-eight hours." Often, that changes the tone.

People who are expecting a fight don't know what to do when you say thank you. Now, do you *feel* thankful? Probably not! It's difficult to be thankful for your critics. But you can still express thanks and model a godly response. Even if their comment was wrong, your gracious response keeps the lines of communication open and avoids severing the relationship.

Ask clarifying questions.

After one Sunday morning service I met a new couple in the lobby. They introduced themselves, and then started in. The lady said, "The music was way too loud! I had to come out in the lobby and watch the service on the TV." Rather than defend our volume, I asked questions. It turned out that we were the fourth church she had visited and in each case the music was too loud. I discovered she had partial hearing loss and was bothered by certain frequencies.

I asked her, "Where were you sitting?" I then directed her to a different place in the room where the frequencies would be less harsh. Her tone and demeanor softened. Then I said, "Try that. If that doesn't work, let me know. We'll have someone sit next to you with a decibel meter and try to figure out what's going on." She and her husband were speechless and stunned. By asking questions, I communicated that I cared for her. She hadn't received that response in the other churches.

Make the necessary changes.

Not all criticism is wrong. Even if it's offered in the wrong spirit, it can still help identify problems. I recently had a guy angrily confront me about problems in our church kitchen. He did it in the wrong way, attacking and exaggerating. But after his rant was over, I carefully considered his complaints. Some of them were valid, so we made the necessary changes. If you disregard criticism anytime it's presented with an unhealthy attitude, you just might miss valid feedback. Be willing to consider that you might be able to learn something despite someone's immaturity.

Check the criticism with your peers.

Review the criticism with others who can help you consider it objectively. Ask them, "Have you observed this? Do I have a blind spot? Is this criticism valid and something I need to address, or is this just someone with an issue?" The people around you can help clarify whether an actual issue exists.

Recently, I told a story about meeting the vice president of the United States. I actually sat in his office and talked with him! It was a life highlight for me, but I told the story carefully, aware that some people might consider my visit a validation of his politics. Despite my carefully chosen words, I received an angry letter of accusation. Before responding, I checked with trusted leaders. I asked them if my statement had appeared political. When none of them agreed with the angry letter writer, I determined that her words simply weren't accurate. I replied to her letter and thanked her for sharing her observations, but made no change.

Even if you weren't in the wrong, apologize.

An apology doesn't mean you have to accept the person's criticism or validate what they said, and it certainly doesn't mean you give them what they want. Instead, an apology acknowledges the perceived offense and gives your critic the chance to forgive and perhaps even apologize themselves! An appropriate apology can be said this way:

- I'm sorry I offended you. Would you forgive me?
- I'm sorry. It wasn't my intent to make you mad. Obviously, I could have communicated better to you.
- Obviously, you feel strongly about this. I'm sorry. Perhaps the Lord is speaking to your heart to be involved in that area of ministry.

Don't let critics distract you from the cause!

That's easy to write, but extremely difficult to do. Criticism hurts. Criticism keeps you from action. Critics are cruel as they hurl their opinions without thought or feeling. Their comments keep you awake at night and distract you from the mission ahead. You spend way too much time focusing on the critic instead of your assignment from God.

Too many leaders try to respond to every criticism instead of turning away and going back to the mission. In the process, they miss numerous opportunities to advance the Kingdom. You can't let critics and complainers control your agenda.

Consider that something negative may be happening in the critic's life.

When people lash out at church or school, it's often because they have a problem at home or work. They feel out of control in one area of their life, so they try to exert control in another area.

Bruce came into my office, shouting at me in anger. I sat there and listened until he didn't have any energy left to keep shouting. Then, rather than directly respond to his angry rant, I asked, "How are you doing, Bruce? What's going on in your life? How can I pray for you today?" He broke down in tears. His marriage was in trouble, and he didn't know what to do. I cried with him, and we prayed together. Before Bruce left, he said, "Pastor Rod, I'm sorry I yelled at you. I didn't mean any of that." Rather than lecture him, I said, "I know, Bruce. I forgive you. Don't worry about that at all. I'm praying for you." Bruce and I are still close friends.

Respond to your critics with love and kindness.

When I became pastor, one of the leaders in our prayer ministry wasn't happy. Clementine didn't like me at all. She became one of my most outspoken critics, both to my face, and more often, behind my back. Rather than respond, I prayed. I sensed the Lord was going to use Clementine's attacks as an opportunity for me to demonstrate patience and sound leadership. In response to her anger, I treated her with love and kindness.

Sometime later, Clementine was visiting family in another part of the country and was hospitalized. I flew to the East Coast, rented a car, and showed up at the hospital. I sat with her for an hour, prayed with her, and then returned to the airport and flew home.

Clementine, my number one critic, became my most faithful prayer partner. When I did right in response to her wrong, she changed.

Pray for your critics.

Some of the best advice Alton gave me when I became pastor was, "Rod, you have to pastor all the people." I've never forgotten that. I pray regularly for my critics—that God will help me love them, forgive them, and have a soft spot in my heart toward them. I refuse to respond to critics in a way that diminishes my leadership or testimony. I remind myself of Jesus' words: "Love your enemies, do good to those who hate you, bless those who curse you, pray for those who mistreat you" (Luke 6:27–28).

I guarantee that if you're doing anything of value, you'll have critics. I can also guarantee that if you're making any effort to grow, you'll need course corrections throughout the journey. When critics emerge, see them as hurting people who need the love and forgiveness of the Master. When a trusted friend or mentor approaches you with a word of correction, receive it with thanks, knowing that "words from a sincere friend are better than many kisses from an enemy" (Proverbs 27:6 NLT). If you need to vent, find a safe, trusted friend. Pour out your feelings and emotions to that person, then respond to your critic in the way Jesus taught.

Stuff to consider . . .

1. Think of a time recently when someone criticized you. How did you respond? Was it a wise response? How could you have handled it differently?

2. Why is it wise to wait before responding to a critic?

3. How can negative events in a person's life turn them into a critic?

4. Will you be implementing a major change soon? Brainstorm all the possible questions, criticisms, and complaints you might receive—then come up with responses for each. If you're going through this with your team, complete the brainstorm as a group.

9

Everyone Wants to Be Treated with Respect

As a kid, I was picked on and bullied. I still remember the pain of being the last person picked in kickball at recess. Standing there, hoping one of the captains will pick you is a lonely feeling. No one wants to hear, "Okay, I guess we'll take Rod since he's all that's left." I know what it's like to feel excluded, left out.

As a senior in high school, I was voted president of the choir. I know, it's not exactly captain of the football team, but I was picked! I was selected first, the leader among my peers. I felt like I was part of a group that mattered, I was included.

Maybe you've been in a situation where you felt left out, like a misfit. It might've been a party where you didn't know anyone, a playground pick where no one wanted you on their team, or sitting alone in church. At that moment, you longed for anyone to acknowledge you, talk to you, and make you feel part of the "club." As a leader, you have the power to include people or exclude people. When you include people, they feel noticed, special, and valuable. When you exclude people, they feel worthless and invisible.

To be an effective leader, you must be an includer. You can't just return the calls of the people you like or meet with the people you enjoy. You must include everyone. An effective leader can't be prejudiced. You must lead *all* people, not just the people like you! To do that, you have to treat all people with respect.

Leaders fall into two categories: inclusive leaders and exclusive leaders. The differences between the two are easily observed. Essentially, an inclusive leader draws many different people around them, while an exclusive leader builds an exclusive club that allows access only to "special" people.

This type of leader [inclusive] consistently points the team to a common goal, a mountain to climb together, a reason for living, working, and following.

What kind of leader are you? I've gathered some useful criteria to help you determine which camp you fall into, as well as to identify leaders you'd like to follow . . . or avoid.

The Differences between Inclusive Leaders and Exclusive Leaders

An exclusive leader is known by what they're against.

Establishing clear expectations is the mark of any good leader, but exclusive leaders often rely on lengthy, complex, and sometimes vague (even unwritten) rules to keep their subordinates under their thumb.

An inclusive leader is known by what they're for.

A more mature, inclusive leader recognizes the need to communicate a few important expectations clearly and then give their followers room to operate in their strengths. They openly appreciate the diverse talents of their team members and champion others' ideas when they align with the vision and culture of the community.

An exclusive leader leads by fighting a common enemy.

An exclusive leader will almost always have an enemy. If there's no real enemy, they invent one. They'll do whatever it takes (and tell you whatever story necessary) to convince you their enemy is also your enemy. Exclusive leaders uniquely understand that people won't follow them on their own merits. Instead, they must find someone for the group to hate together, someone to exclude. This is a favorite tactic of playground bullies. When you spot it in someone you're following or thinking of following, run for the hills! It won't be long until that leader is rallying people against *you*.

An inclusive leader leads by pursuing a common goal.

On the other hand, an inclusive leader understands there will be enemies in life but chooses not to use them as tools to lead others. Instead, this type of leader consistently points the team to a common goal, a mountain to climb together, a reason for living, working, and following.

An exclusive leader continually reviews past hurts to keep the common enemy hated and excluded.

The exclusive leader can't afford for followers to forget the offense of the past. If they forget, they might quit following. This leader understands that the strength of their own convictions is insufficient to attract followers. They keep a record of wrongs and play it often. And . . . with each playing, the story grows.

An inclusive leader puts past hurts behind to keep the goal in focus.

An inclusive leader understands that resentment will stop the growth of an organization, family, relationship, or church. Instead, this type of leader acknowledges the hurt and then decides that the goal still matters and the hurt must be left behind—and kept off the record book.

Like a soldier who jumps on top of a grenade to keep his comrades from suffering harm, an inclusive leader absorbs the worst impact of a hurt to avoid passing its toxic effects along to their followers.

An exclusive leader leads by fear and intimidation.

Followers of an exclusive leader will rarely challenge the assertions of the leader. They understand because they've seen it happen to others: If you challenge the leader, you're out, excluded. Then your wrongs will be recorded and reported. The culture generated under this type of leadership is low in creativity and morale as followers avoid voicing even legitimate concerns or new ideas for fear of rocking the boat.

An inclusive leader leads by love and acceptance.

Inclusive leaders are realistic about their own faults and the faults of others. They choose to love and accept people despite their shortcomings. They keep no record of wrongs. This leadership style establishes a culture where followers respect, but do not fear their leader. As a result, they can ask questions without anxiety of being ridiculed, accept correction more readily, and feel empowered to take greater risks.

An exclusive leader makes those outside their circle feel targeted.

Those who follow an exclusive leader feel this way: "If I'm not with them, they're talking about me." Little is as frightening for them as being outside the circle of the exclusive leader. As the leader rallies their troops against you, it's easy to convince yourself the entire world is against you. The result of this kind of leadership is simply dehumanizing. Under a sense of constant threat, followers want to be in the dysfunctional circle, so they won't be the target. They tolerate the mistreatment of others because they feel they're safe as long as someone else is in the crosshairs. This kind of behavior, initiated by the leader, is a dangerous cycle.

> **The inclusive leader has a way of noticing those who are on the outside.**

An inclusive leader makes those outside their circle feel welcomed.

The inclusive leader has a way of noticing those who are on the outside. Theirs is a constantly evolving and changing circle. The phrase we often use in the organization I lead is "enlarge your circle of love." An inclusive leader loves to see someone else come into the fold. Teams thrive under this type of leadership. Individuals desire to help one another and see each other grow because there's no danger of being marginalized just because someone else performs well.

An exclusive leader always has a target for their anger.

There will always be someone or something against them. This kind of leader is always a victim and always mad at someone.

They often develop "targets of opportunity." You may become a target just because you're available.

An inclusive leader always has a target for their love.

The inclusive leader always has a project; someone they're helping, someone they can identify as the target to add to their circle. They can't wait to see that person touched by love.

An exclusive leader has a scarcity mentality.

The exclusive leader acts as if there's a limited supply of love, money, grace, perks . . . whatever the case may be. They believe if someone else gets something, it's costing them, so they have to keep others out. Unfortunately, the exclusive leader often succeeds so completely in keeping people out that they no longer have a community to share anything with at all.

> **Everyone has the potential to help the team get to the goal.**

An inclusive leader has an abundance mentality.

The inclusive leader understands there's more than enough to go around, so they're generous with their time and resources, investing not only in their teams, but also in leaders younger or less experienced than themselves. They rejoice in the blessings of others because they're convinced of an unlimited supply. Because they share generously with others, others share generously with them. You won't find this kind of leader wanting for followers, no matter what kind of season they're walking through.

An exclusive leader focuses on the faults and failures of others.

This is partly to make sure the focus stays off their own faults and failures. It also ensures there's always a potential enemy on the horizon. Everyone has the potential to one day be on the excluded list, and the exclusive leader keeps a record for future reference.

An inclusive leader focuses on the strengths and potential of others.

Why? Because the mission is all-important. Everyone has the potential to help the team get to the goal. The inclusive leader wants to draw out that potential and see it used for the advantage of the entire group.

An exclusive leader's motto is: "We don't need anyone else."

The exclusive leader isn't interested in quantity. To this person, it's more fun for the inner group to be together with no intrusion from anyone else. The thought is: *There's just no more room in our circle.*

An inclusive leader's motto is: "There's always room for one more."

The inclusive leader believes the more, the merrier. There's always room to enlarge the circle, always room for one more person in the group.

An exclusive leader is motivated by insecurity.

An exclusive leader truly believes people won't see their faults and failures if they magnify the faults of others. They fear someone will discover their weaknesses or inadequacies, so they'll do anything to avoid detection or admission. They exclude and expose others, so they won't be excluded or exposed.

An inclusive leader is motivated by mission.

To the inclusive leader, the mission is all-important. They'll candidly admit their weaknesses in hopes that someone else will surface with corresponding strengths. Why? So the entire team can all get there together. So they can all climb the mountain together.

An exclusive leader can only lead a few.

Why? Because it takes a lot of time and effort to keep everyone galvanized against the common enemy. The exclusive leader must continually monitor others to make sure they aren't accidentally saying nice things about the opposition—or worse, seeing the truth and turning against the inner group. But it's terribly difficult to keep a large group deceived over time.

An inclusive leader can lead many.

The cause is just. The mission is understood. Followers want others to join them on the journey. The inclusive leader is only limited in the number of people they can lead by the number of inclusive leaders who work under and alongside them.

An exclusive leader is marked by bitterness.

By now, it should be obvious. An exclusive leader is a bitter person. The process of keeping people angry saps the joy and vitality out of a person. It's hard work to keep record of wrongs.

An inclusive leader is marked by forgiveness.

The inclusive leader knows the cost of not forgiving and fears it. The cost is bitterness (Hebrews 12:15), a hard heart, and ultimately, not being forgiven by God (Matthew 18:35). The price is too high.

An exclusive leader has followers for a season.

People move in and out of favor with the exclusive leader. They can't stay in it for long because of the intensity. Exclusive leaders always have an inner circle, but different people may be in it at different times—and someone else is now excluded.

An inclusive leader has followers for a lifetime.

There's always room to invest in one more life, one more ministry, or one more mission. The inclusive leader attracts mission-minded, life-long followers.

> **There's always room to invest in one more life, one more ministry, or one more mission.**

An exclusive leader avoids personal sacrifice.

Exclusive leaders often refuse to sacrifice preference. Their way is the right way. Anyone who suggests another way becomes the next enemy, and the cycle continues.

An inclusive leader will pay any price to achieve the goal.

The mission, the goal, matters so much that an inclusive leader will model paying a high price. They understand: the higher the goal, the higher the cost.

An exclusive leader uses people.

The key word is *manipulation*. The exclusive leader sees people as tools to achieve the leader's personal agenda.

An inclusive leader loves people.

The key word is *motivation*. The inclusive leader sees people as potential team members who can come along on the journey.

An exclusive leader ends life alone.

It is the inevitable end. The exclusive leader dies bitter and alone. When they lose their ability to rail against and rally others against an enemy, there's no reason for others to follow them. When they become old and feeble, there's no longer a reason for people to fear them. Instead, people ignore them.

An inclusive leader ends life loved.

An inclusive leader has invested in the lives of many people who are continually seeking a way to thank them. At the end of their lives, though they may be old and feeble, people still seek their wisdom and advice.

The biblical model of an exclusive leader is Satan.

Satan started as an exclusive leader. He led a rebellion in heaven because he wanted worship directed to him rather than to God. Later, Satan tempted Eve by convincing her that God was excluding her. Satan tricked her into thinking that if she ate from the fruit of the tree, she would have the same knowledge as God.

Satan started as an exclusive leader, and he continues in that pattern today. It's the trick he uses against us. We call it *condemnation*.

Satan keeps a record of everything you've done wrong and reminds you about it as often as possible. He wants you to feel worthless. He wants you to feel useless. He wants you to believe that God could never forgive you or use you. He wants to convince you that you're the only person who has ever been so bad. The Bible calls Satan the "accuser of our brothers and sisters" (Revelation 12:10, NLT). He accuses you of every bad thing you've done or thought. He attempts to use the wrongs in your life as a barrier to forgiveness. Satan has a plan for your life.

He wants to isolate you from others by encouraging you to harbor bitterness and unforgiveness toward them. He reminds you of the wrongs others have committed against you and the hurts you've suffered. Satan is the ultimate exclusive leader. Why does he do all this? His goal is to steal, to kill, and to destroy. He wants to steal your joy, your ministry, your marriage, and your family. He wants to kill your spirit and destroy your faith in God.

> **Jesus doesn't seek to exclude anyone. He's the ultimate inclusive leader.**

The biblical model of an inclusive leader is Jesus.

Jesus doesn't seek to exclude anyone. He's the ultimate inclusive leader. In fact, the Bible says He's our *advocate* before the Father (1 John 2:1).

See the difference? Satan is an accuser. He wants you to remember all the wrongs you've done—and he doesn't want God to forget them either. In contrast, Jesus is an advocate. He stands before God on your behalf. He says, "Father, I want you to include them and forgive them. Not because of who they are, but because of the sacrifice I made and the price I paid." He wanted so badly to include you that He died for you. Why did He do it? "For God so loved the world that he gave his one and only Son, that whoever believes in him shall not perish but have eternal life" (John 3:16).

Imagine that! Jesus loved you so much He died for you. He wanted to include you in heaven, for eternity. He wanted to include you so much that He made the ultimate sacrifice—His life. And He included everyone! "And everyone who calls on the name of the Lord will be saved" (Acts 2:21).

Jesus wanted to include you so much He was willing to sacrifice His life to include you, and He wants you to include others so much that He made the forgiveness of your sin dependent upon your willingness to forgive them. Jesus said: "If you forgive other people when they sin against you, your Heavenly Father will also forgive you. But if you do not forgive others their sins, your Father will not forgive your sins" (Matthew 6:14–15).

That's good motivation not to keep track of the wrongs of others. I want to be forgiven! And, thankfully, our Heavenly Father is willing to forgive. Can you imagine if every evil thing, every thought, every word you ever said was played on a screen? None of us would want to see that. God gave us a simple plan: forgiveness.

While Satan's plan for your life is "to steal and kill and destroy," Jesus' plan is "that [you] may have life and have it to the full" (John 10:10). His forgiveness of our sins—and our forgiveness of others for the wrongs they've committed against us—opens the door to the full life Jesus' sacrificial death makes available to us.

Stuff to think about . . .

1. Take a few minutes and make a list of leaders you've observed and decide whether they're exclusive leaders or inclusive leaders.

2. Why do exclusive leaders need to keep a common enemy in focus?

3. Why do people love and admire an inclusive leader?

4. What steps can you take to become a more inclusive leader?

10

Great Leaders Are Willing to Sacrifice Their Rights

One of the most interesting stories in the Bible is found in the first three chapters of John. An amazing leader, John the Baptist attracted multitudes of followers, but he told his followers, "You think I'm good? Just wait. There is one coming after me who is amazing. I'm not even worthy to tie His shoes!"

One day when John saw Jesus walking toward him, John declared to his followers: "Look, the Lamb of God, who takes away the sin of the world!" (John 1:29).

The next day John was with two of his disciples when Jesus passed by. Again, John said, "Look, the Lamb of God!" (John 1:36). That day, something different happened. "When the two disciples heard him say this, they followed Jesus" (1:37).

The Bible doesn't tell us who both of these guys were (1:40), but if they were getting personal attention from John, they were likely some of his key leaders—two people he had poured his life into. Suddenly they chose to leave him and follow Jesus.

It hurts when people leave. I don't care what someone tells you, it hurts. When a valued team member leaves your business, it hurts. When a customer posts a negative review that says she's never coming back, it hurts. When people leave the church, it hurts.

I don't know what made me think of it, but the other day I started thinking about all the people who have left the church in my more than fifteen years as pastor. It was discouraging to realize that I could fill a church (maybe more than one!) with the people who have left.

No one likes losing people. I've had leaders tell me, "I don't care. Let them go." I can tell you that's usually the mark of leaders who have become callous toward the people they lead—which is a dangerous place to be—or it's a lie to mask the hurt. In either case, those leaders just aren't comfortable admitting their pain.

As heartrending as it can be to see someone walk away, you can handle it without falling into a deep depression by recognizing that when someone leaves the church, it's for one of only two reasons.

Number one: They aren't supposed to be there. My leadership team knows that the Spirit of the Lord is not enshrined at 4501 Burrow Drive in North Little Rock, Arkansas. Sometimes a person leaves to bless—or be blessed by—the ministry of another church. Sometimes a person must leave for the protection of our church. If that's the case, we don't want to keep them here. We bless them as they go and say goodbye.

Number two: They are missing God's will and plan for their lives. In that case, we pray for them. But, regardless of why they leave, it hurts.

As the third chapter of John unfolds, Jesus was gaining followers and John was losing followers. John's ministry was growing smaller every day. Some of his remaining followers finally approached him to express concern:

They came to John and said to him, "Rabbi, that man who was with you on the other side of the Jordan—the one you testified about—look, he is baptizing, and everyone is going to him." (John 3:26)

John's response is one of the most powerful passages in the entire Bible:

To this John replied, "A person can receive only what is given them from heaven. You yourselves can testify that I said, 'I am not the Messiah but am sent ahead of him.' The bride belongs to the bridegroom. The friend who attends the bridegroom waits and listens for him and is full of joy when he hears the bridegroom's voice. That joy is mine, and it is now complete. He must become greater; I must become less." (John 3:27-30)

The King James Version says it this way: "He must increase, but I must decrease." My way of saying it is, "There must be more of Jesus and less of me."

There's no doubt about it, in our world, Jesus must increase. We need more of Him. Our days are inundated with reminders of just how much we need Him. We hear about war, recession, depression, natural disasters, nuclear threats, sexual harassment, opiate addiction, and human trafficking. Our world and our nation need more of Jesus.

It's easy to get excited at the idea of Jesus increasing. Great old-time Pentecostal preachers can camp on that one phrase and bring a crowd to its feet: "Jesus must increase." But there's a second part to that verse, one we really don't like to discuss much. John said, "He must increase—I *must* decrease" or, "I must become less." John was saying, "There must be more of Jesus and less of John." "I must decrease" has not been the rallying cry of the church in recent years. We're all about superstar preachers, hotshot worship leaders, and television stars. We've made our own names famous rather than pointing others to the name that is above all names. When you believe Jesus is the way, the truth, and the life, you recognize the need—and, indeed, the honor—of moving aside to turn the focus on Him. Like John, you see clearly one of the simplest truths of all: To reach a world that desperately needs Jesus, "He must increase, I must decrease."

To reach a world that desperately needs Jesus, "He must increase, I must decrease."

That one truth, if truly embraced by leaders, business groups, and churches, could rock our world. Can you imagine what might happen if you really decided it wasn't about you and me, but about Him? Can you imagine the difference if what you liked, preferred, and wanted wasn't the central issue, but the primary objective was to see Jesus increase? What kind of impact would a person, a church, or a business like that make?

John could have told his followers, "You're right. We must do something about this Jesus guy. I am John the *Baptist.* Baptism is my deal. We've got to get bigger and better. We've got to win. After all, we did this first."

With ideas like that, John would have ended with this statement: "I have my rights." Instead, he said, "I must become less."

John the Baptist was willing to sacrifice his rights, preferences, and fame so people would know Jesus.

I want to be like that. More of Jesus, less of me. I want to impact a world. I want to point a generation to Jesus. If that's going to happen, if we're going to change our world, we must focus on the second half of the equation: "I must decrease."

Decreasing hurts. It means giving up your rights. It means putting Jesus before you. Becoming less is a decision; it doesn't happen accidentally. You must choose to become less.

How do you become less so Jesus becomes more? For that to happen, you must give up some rights. It's a tough truth about leadership: *Leaders must sacrifice their rights.* In fact, if you want to increase your leadership potential, examine what rights you can give up voluntarily—before it's required.

Have you ever heard someone say, "Hey, I have my rights!"? That's not a leadership statement. That statement is all about the person, not about Jesus. Leaders sacrifice their rights. If you want to become less, let me encourage you to start by giving up these rights.

Leaders Give Up Their Rights

Leaders give up the right to be a jerk.

Leaders, by definition, have followers. As a leader, someone follows everything you do and every action you take. In every situation you must keep in mind that someone will copy your behavior. One of my mentors, Alton Garrison, used to tell me, "Everyone can be a jerk, but us." When you're a jerk, you devalue your testimony and harm the cause of Christ.

My good friend David is service manager at a car dealership. One day when I went to the dealership I couldn't find David. The staff said he was there somewhere, but no one knew exactly where. I came back later, and David apologized. He said, "I'm sorry you couldn't find me, Rod. I was hiding behind my desk."

I was curious. Service managers don't usually hide. David said, "Do you know that guy from our church, Clarence? Every time he comes in, I hide. He's the biggest jerk I know. He's everyone's least favorite customer. He is rude, demanding, and loud. I'm not afraid of him. We have other rude customers. But, what I am afraid of is that he will recognize me, and my staff will hear that he goes to my church. I don't want anyone to know we go to the same church. No one would want to attend our church."

As a leader, you give up the right to be a jerk. Someone is always watching!

As a leader, you give up the right to be a jerk. Someone is always watching! My wife won't even let me honk when someone cuts me off in traffic. She says, "Rod, they might recognize you. Act right."

You might think, *But you don't know what that person did. They were a jerk first!* It doesn't matter. You represent your company, or your church. When you are a jerk, your whole team suffers. You'll never know the people who avoid you because you are a jerk. Jerks don't attract new business. Jerks don't lead winning teams. Jerks don't lead people to Jesus. How do you know if you're a jerk?

- Jerks say what they think without regard for the feelings of others.
- Jerks put their own interests before the good of others.
- Jerks throw temper tantrums.
- Jerks demand their own way and become angry if it doesn't happen.
- Jerks assume the worst of others.
- Jerks build themselves up and tear others down.
- Jerks evaluate others, but are unwilling to evaluate themselves.
- Jerks are not willing to admit their weaknesses.
- Jerks are proud, selfish, and haughty.

Paul's description of love leaves no room for jerks. He said: "It is not rude; it is not self-seeking, it is not provoked [nor overly sensitive and easily angered]" (1 Corinthians 13:5, AMP).

If you want Jesus to increase, don't be a jerk!

Leaders give up the right to lose control.

Leaders can't get mad, lose their cool, or hurl accusations, anger, and insults. If they do, they limit their ability to lead. People will never forget the times you lose your cool. Unfortunately, they'll never follow you with the same commitment again. Remember this principle: When you lose your temper, you lose.

The Bible has a lot to say about anger and self-control:

- A gentle answer turns away wrath, but a harsh word stirs up anger. (Proverbs 15:1)

- But the fruit of the Spirit is love, joy, peace, forbearance, kindness, goodness, faithfulness, gentleness and self-control. Against such things there is no law. (Galatians 5:22–23)
- Like a city whose walls are broken through is a person who lacks self-control. (Proverbs 25:28)

Years ago, I played golf with a well-known pastor. He led a good church, was well-known in our state, and held a leadership position in his denomination. We were having a wonderful time until the thirteenth hole, where he hooked his drive out of bounds. He didn't say anything. He just put another ball down and took a second, harder swing. This time, the ball didn't go out of bounds but went into the woods. Again, he was quiet. When he got to his ball, he had an opening to hit it through the trees but he missed. The ball rebounded off a tree and flew behind him. That was it. He couldn't take it anymore. I watched as this respected leader slammed his seven iron into the trunk of the tree and started yelling and cussing at the tree. I felt a little sorry for the tree. That pastor didn't talk to me for the rest of that hole or the next. He just stomped around and, by the way, wrote a wrong score on the scorecard.

I never played golf with him again—and, what's more, I lost all respect for him. That day, his actions disqualified him as a leader I was willing to follow. If he got that mad at a tree, I couldn't imagine what he would do to a person!

Leaders give up the right to lose their temper. You might say, "But Rod, that's just my personality! I've got red hair. I'm Irish." I suggest you change your personality with the help of the Holy

Spirit, who gives us a spirit of "power, love, and *self-discipline*" (2 Timothy 1:7, my emphasis).

A businesswoman once told me, "I've learned, if you want to get results, you have to get mad." I looked at her and replied, "But the results you get aren't worth the respect you lose."

Losing your temper is all about you and nothing about Jesus. Remember the goal: "More of Jesus, less of me."

Leaders give up the right to "take a break" from their role.

There's hardly a moment when leaders are not aware of the responsibility of leadership. That doesn't sound like a sacrifice, but it is. What if I don't feel like going to church one Sunday? What if I want to stay home or play golf? What if I want to go to another church? I don't have that option. I have a responsibility to the people following me and to the organization I serve.

> **Losing your temper is all about you and nothing about Jesus.**

If you're a leader, that applies in every area of your life. You can't check out of your leadership position at school, at work, or at a restaurant. If you're a leader, you're a leader—*all the time*. Regardless of the time or place, your actions reflect on your business, your team, your church, and most importantly, on Jesus!

My boys and I have always enjoyed attending sporting events together, but the part we can't stand is all the traffic and searching for a parking spot before the game. Years ago, when my older son, Tyler, was ten years old, we were in Dallas for Christmas and had good seats for a Dallas Mavericks game. Tyler was super excited and wanted to get there early.

He went online to look for the best place to park and decided we should park in the Hooter's parking lot and take the Hooter's shuttle to the game. He said, "Let's go early, park at Hooter's, eat at Hooter's, and ride the Hooter's shuttle. After the game, they'll take us right back."

As we sat in traffic together, I used the opportunity to teach him an important lesson. I said, "Son, we can't go to Hooter's. It wouldn't look right. I want to avoid every appearance of wrong. What would people think if they saw the pastor at Hooter's?"

Tyler answered, "Come on Dad. This isn't Little Rock. We're in Dallas. Who will see us here?" At that precise moment, a church bus from First Assembly of God in Malvern, Arkansas—full of people we knew, waving their arms off and shouting hello—stopped at the light next to us. What a great teachable moment! As a leader, no matter where you are, you're always "on."

Paul told his young protégé Timothy: "Preach the word; be prepared in season and out of season" (2 Timothy 4:2). In other words—always be ready to represent Jesus.

Leaders give up the right to have things the way they want them.

Everyone has preferences, but leaders understand that not only are preferences often irrelevant, they can also limit and distract from the mission.

Years ago, I spent eighteen months as the worship leader at our church. That's not my primary gift, but I love to worship and I accepted the assignment. For that year and a half, I led the church in a whole lot of songs I didn't like. In fact, every service, we sang something I didn't enjoy.

Why? Because when I accepted the assignment, I gave up the right to sing only the songs I liked. I had to lead everyone: the people who liked modern worship choruses, the people who liked old choruses, and the people who liked hymns. It didn't matter what I liked. What mattered was that everyone worshipped God.

Paul wrote:

> If you have any encouragement from being united with Christ, if any comfort from his love, if any common sharing in the Spirit, if any tenderness and compassion, then make my joy complete by being like-minded, having the same love, being one in spirit and of one mind. Do nothing out of selfish ambition or vain conceit. Rather, in humility value others above yourselves, not looking to your own interests but each of you to the interests of the others. (Philippians 2:1–4)

If you're a leader, it doesn't really matter what you like. In fact, what you like is probably irrelevant. What matters is what is right. And what *is* right? Whatever focuses attention squarely on Jesus.

John the Baptist probably felt a few twinges of pain when his followers left him to follow Jesus. Though it didn't feel good, he knew it was right. That's why he continued to point people to Jesus.

Leaders give up the right to demand attention.

This is the hard part. If Jesus must increase and you must decrease, that means people are going to know His name more than yours. Something inside each of us makes us desire recognition, attention, position, and fame. I hate that part of me. If your goal is becoming less, you'll learn to hate that part of you, too. Paul, who was arguably more qualified than *any* of us to boast in his own accomplishments, summed up a perfect solution for us: "May I never boast except in the cross of our Lord Jesus Christ, through which the world has been crucified to me, and I to the world" (Galatians 6:14).

> If Jesus must increase and you must decrease, that means people are going to know His name more than yours.

Leaders who insist on being the star cause problems. We've had enough stars—and seen way too many of them fall. How annoying and immature are kids when they fight for attention? They remind me of leaders who seek attention for themselves. This what you need to understand: It's not about you—it's about Jesus. The question is, Are you willing to stop your childish efforts to get attention and give the attention to Him?

I'm blessed to lead a hundred-year-old church. On the wall in a main hallway of our church hangs a large plaque that reads, "May those who follow find us faithful." I like that. It's a constant reminder that we are temporary bearers—not originators or owners—of God's truth. There were generations before us, and there will be generations after us, all entrusted with bearing God's truth, and I want to set them up for success by being faithful to God's call in my lifetime. I pray often: "More of Jesus, less of Rod. Lord, I want Your name to be known, not mine. Let there be more of Jesus in this place and less of us."

Leaders give up the right to set their own schedules.

I sometimes attend things that aren't enjoyable, convenient, or fun because it's the price of leadership. I want to lend my support to every area that makes a kingdom difference, whether it's a personal favorite or not.

Years ago, I planned a golf trip to Palm Springs, California. Eleven other guys were going with me, but I did all the planning. It was going to be an amazing trip! The day before we were supposed to leave, a key leader in our church passed away. I knew I had no choice. I stayed home and performed the funeral, while the other guys went and had a fun time playing golf. You know what? I never told the man's family I was missing my vacation. That didn't matter. As a leader, I understand my schedule is not my own.

Years later, it happened again. Cindy and I were going to Palm Springs, California. The day before our trip, an elderly gentleman in our church died. We were close to the family, and I knew I had to stay. Once again, I cancelled the trip and never told his family.

Cindy and I still haven't made it to Palm Springs. We're afraid if we try to schedule another trip there, someone else will die!

You can't schedule crises. People don't die on your convenient timetable. Students don't schedule teachable moments around your family time. Plans will change. You will miss flights, vacations, appointments—even some games, recitals, and practices. That's just part of being a leader. Leaders understand that their schedules must be flexible. As a leader, you give up the right to always do what you want. It doesn't matter what you want. What matters? What is right.

Leaders give up the right to speak their minds.

No doubt you know someone who speaks before they think. Annie is that way. She opens her mouth and lets hurtful words fly, on a regular basis. Her excuse is, "Well, I just tell it like it is." The problem is, she is often wrong and ends up wounding others. Annie is not a leader and never will be because she is unwilling to give up that ill-chosen right.

As a leader, your words carry more weight than other people's words. How many wounded people lie in the wake of the leader who "tells it like it is"! You must think before you speak or act. You can't pop off. You can't just say what you think. Solomon, one of the wisest men who ever lived wrote: "A fool gives full vent to his anger, but a wise man holds it in check" (Proverbs 29:11 HCSB). You have to ask yourself, "What is the right thing to say? What will make Jesus increase?"

> **As a leader, your words carry more weight than other people's words.**

Paul offered this guidance: "Let your conversation be always full of grace, seasoned with salt, so that you may know how to answer everyone" (Colossians 4:6). In writing to the Philippians, he asked the believers to be "like-minded, having the same love, being one in spirit and of one mind" (Philippians 2:2). Instead of just speaking your mind, try to speak words that bring unity, promote love, and produce joy!

Leaders give up the right to pout.

The dictionary definition of pout is "to look or be sullen." Pouting is a visible way to let people know you are unhappy because you didn't get your way. The goal of pouting is to make sure everyone around you knows you're unhappy, and it's one of the most selfish things you can do. It's all about getting attention for yourself. People pout over things like these:

- Someone else got chosen for the solo.
- Your microphone wasn't on.
- Your office is smaller than your coworker's.
- Your announcement got left out of the newsletter.
- The room wasn't set up the way you wanted it.

Face it. Things go wrong. When they do, you have a choice: pout or act like a mature adult and get over it.

My wife and I had a rule in our house: "No pouting." If the boys pouted, the punishment was their choice: Get a spanking or go to bed. Tyler and Parker quickly learned not to whine and pout.

The Book of Hebrews illustrates a powerful alternative to pouting:

> But recall the former days in which, after you were illuminated, you endured a great struggle with sufferings; partly while you were made a spectacle both by reproaches and tribulations, and partly while you became companions of those who were so treated; for you had compassion on me in my chains, and joyfully accepted the plundering of your goods, knowing that you have a better and an enduring possession for yourselves in heaven. (Hebrews 10:32-34, NKJV)

Can you imagine? Even though they faced abuse, humiliation, hardship, suffering, and the loss of their belongings, they maintained an attitude of joy. You read that and wonder, *How were they able to do it?* They kept a joy filled-attitude because their focus was on heaven!

You can lead without whining and pouting because you have something better waiting for you in heaven.

Leaders give up the right to ignore the rules.

When my son Tyler was five years old, he was riding with me on the highway. Suddenly the radar detector on my dashboard started beeping. I quickly hit the brakes and slowed down.

Tyler asked, "Dad, what's that sound?"

I calmly gave him one of those oversimplified, above-his-head, grown-up answers designed to placate curiosity without really answering the question. "It's a police finder."

Tyler, full of curiosity, innocently persisted. "Why do you have a police finder?"

"I like to know if police are nearby."

"Why?" Tyler continued the inquisition.

I fumbled for a good explanation. "Well, I might want to stop and greet them, or wave, or . . . buy them a soda or something."

My son just kept asking why until I finally told him the truth: "Son, that beeping is to warn me to slow down when I'm breaking the law so I won't get a ticket. Dad has been a bad example today. I'm sorry."

I took the radar detector off my dashboard and threw it in the trash. I wanted Tyler to follow my rules, but I was a rule-breaker myself. That decision made it difficult to lead my son.

My other son Parker got into trouble in a class at our church. When the teacher tried to discipline him, he replied, "I'm the pastor's son. You can't tell me what to do." Parker learned a painful lesson that day about following the rules, regardless of who you are or your position.

What leaders do in moderation, followers will do in excess. I get frustrated when leaders want special privileges. Instead, leaders should say, "I'm going to follow the rules *more* strictly, so people won't abuse the system." If you ignore the rules as a leader, everyone else will choose anarchy. Being a leader doesn't mean getting a pass on the rules; it means following them more closely! That's another biblical principle!

> Let everyone be subject to the governing authorities, for there is no authority except that which God has established. The authorities that exist have been established by God. Consequently, whoever rebels against the authority is rebelling against what God has instituted, and those who do so will bring judgment on themselves. (Romans 13:1-2)

Leaders give up the right to "be me."

Years ago, as one of our pastors and I rode in the car, we discussed the message he had preached the night before. It wasn't very good, so I offered a few thoughts and suggested changes. He replied, "Well, I just have to be me. The congregation will have to accept me for who I am. I shouldn't have to change for them."

"I just have to be me" is a classic excuse for refusing to change or grow. You might as well say, "I don't want to improve."

You won't find "I have to be me" in Scripture. It isn't part of God's plan. His plan is for you to grow every day and become more like Jesus—and less like yourself! Though our souls are saved the moment we accept Christ, the Holy Spirit continues to transform our character and nature throughout our lives. Paul made this clear when he told the believers in Philippi that "he who began a good work in you *will carry it on* to completion" (Philippians 1:6, emphasis added). That's why he implored them to "*continue* to work out your salvation with fear and trembling" (Philippians 2:12, emphasis added).

Anyone who says, "I just have to be me," is saying "more of me, less of Jesus" instead of "more of Jesus, less of me."

If there's something about me that diminishes my ability to represent Christ, I'll change it in a heartbeat. My personal preferences, personality quirks, or fashion choices will never mean more to me than representing Him. *He* must increase. Paul said it this way: "I have become all things to all people so that by all possible means I might save some. I do all this for the sake of the gospel, that I may share in its blessings" (1 Corinthians 9:22–23).

During our midweek service, you won't find me quietly sipping coffee with the adults or calmly listening to a sermon. You're more likely to find me in our student ministry area playing air hockey with a middle schooler or talking to a high school junior about her upcoming ACT. It's not because I like the music or the fashion trends—it's because I believe this young generation will carry the gospel to the ends of the earth and I want to support them in every way possible. I've learned to like things I don't like. It's not about me—it's for the sake of the gospel.

Sacrifice things you want . . . for the sake of the gospel.

Let the Holy Spirit change your personality . . . for the sake of the gospel.

Be willing to do whatever it takes . . . for the sake of the gospel.

Stuff to consider . . .

1. Go back through this chapter and mark the rights you tend to enjoy—perhaps too much.

2. Think how these rights have affected your leadership and the people you lead.

3. Ask the Lord to show you which right is most detrimental to you and others, and commit to give it up.

4. Share your struggle with a trusted friend or mentor and ask for accountability.

5. Examine ways you can lay down your rights.

6. If you're going through this book with your team, discuss whether you as a group have a "rights" culture and how you might improve.

Epilogue

Sometimes, even when you're doing everything right as a leader, things fall apart. That happened to me while writing this book. An unexpected challenge shook me and my wife, Cindy. This book is about the stuff you won't learn from leadership experts. But this portion of the book is about some powerful lessons I learned from hardship and trouble. As we walked through it, I journaled my thoughts and feelings, hopeful that I might gain new understanding about the Lord and His help in times of trouble. I pray this honest, inside look at our journey will encourage you.

As you lead and serve, you not only deal with problems at work or church, you also experience personal challenges and difficulties. In fact, that's often what makes facing the other problems so difficult. You can't stop life. You can't press pause in one area while you tend to the other—though I've wished I could more than once! Instead, you walk through it all simultaneously, sometimes facing significant difficulties on multiple fronts. That's exactly where Cindy and I found ourselves in the spring of 2017.

On Friday, March 31, 2017, I skipped lunch to get away from the office. I was going through a particularly difficult and stressful time, and needed to clear my head. I went to the driving range by myself and hit golf balls, thinking about nothing but the golf ball and where it went.

After a while, I realized I had left my phone on a bench by the pro shop. I walked back and picked it up. When I looked down at my phone, I noticed I had missed a call from Cindy. I called her back, and when she answered, I could tell immediately something was wrong.

> **Even when the news is bad, God is good.**

Cindy said, "The doctor's office called with the results of my test. They said they wanted you to come with me for a follow-up appointment. I told them, 'Rod doesn't usually come to my doctor's appointments. Just tell me now what you're going to tell us at the appointment.' "

When they hesitated, Cindy said, "Just go ahead and tell me. Do they think it's cancer?" The nurse said, "Yes. It appears you have renal cell carcinoma—cancer in your kidney. We need you and Rod to come meet with the surgeon." Then, Cindy said three words that rocked my world: "I have cancer."

Those three words began a journey of growth and discovery for both of us. One of the first things I realized was that trouble often comes when you're in the middle of other troubles. That's not very encouraging, is it? At the time of Cindy's diagnosis, I wasn't at a place of great strength. I was under attack and already fighting a battle, when more trouble came.

But I've also learned that just because another difficult circumstance happens to you, that doesn't mean God has abandoned you. Now, Satan would love for you to think that. That's just how he works. There are times when he comes after you with everything he's got. Please, don't stop reading now. I want to share some of the most important things I learned as we walked through this difficult challenge. I promise, the story gets better and more encouraging!

The Lord is faithful.

Immediately after hearing Cindy's diagnosis I began to pray, asking God for strength and healing and peace. As I prayed, I sensed one thing in my spirit: *The Lord is faithful.* When I got back to my office, I posted that as my Facebook status. No explanation. No story. Just four words: The Lord is faithful.

That became my theme for the next month, and my daily thought: *The Lord is faithful.* Those four words were more powerful than the three words, "I have cancer." The Lord is faithful despite circumstances. He's faithful despite cancer. When things are going well, the Lord is faithful. When life takes an unexpected turn for the worse, the Lord is faithful. You can't always choose the events that come into your life, but you can always choose your response. Even when the news is bad, God is good.

Don't let trouble keep you from fulfilling God's assignment for you.

When Cindy and I were finally able to sit together and talk about the situation, we agreed, "If this is what we've got, then let's deal with it." There was no use feeling sorry for ourselves or trying to figure out a way around it. We wanted to deal with it head-on. We talked about possible treatments, the timing, our schedule, and what events Cindy could miss. Suddenly our calendar didn't seem so important.

We made two decisions that first night. First, Cindy decided we shouldn't try to keep her diagnosis a secret; instead, we would walk through it openly, in community with our church family and our friends. That's not really my nature. I tend to internalize problems and face things on my own. Because there's so much I deal with, I've learned to compartmentalize and keep going. But Cindy felt strongly that we should share the journey. She reasoned that we have many friends who have faced cancer and humbly given us the honor of walking with them through one of the most challenging times of their lives. We knew that we couldn't keep this to ourselves.

It seems like every week, someone in our church or a friend in ministry receives a difficult medical diagnosis. And at some point, in life everyone faces difficult, unexpected circumstances. Maybe you have cancer or another disease. Perhaps someone close to you has died, or your kids are in trouble. Maybe you're facing unexpected financial hardship—you've lost your job, you have bills beyond what you can pay, or you're facing major repairs on your home or car. Maybe it's a divorce or another heartache. No one is immune from trouble, but we get through the trouble better together.

Second, Cindy decided we wouldn't miss any ministry opportunities. I had committed to speak at a conference for children's pastors and workers from around the country just a few weeks after her diagnosis. Cindy was determined I honor that assignment. She didn't want me to miss a Sunday, cancel a speaking engagement, or change my schedule. Her thought was: *Cancer won't stop us from ministry or fulfilling God's purpose. If it does, then cancer wins. And, regardless of what's ahead, I refuse to let cancer win.*

I understand, some illnesses and unexpected life events do disrupt our normal activities and force a change of pace—but they can't sideline us from accomplishing God's purpose for us. You may be in the middle of a trial, but you're still a child of God. When the road gets rough, when the future is uncertain, when you feel like you've been benched, ask the Lord to open your eyes to His purpose for you in that season. His plans for you are good.

Remember, even in times of trouble—*especially* in times of trouble—God has an assignment and a purpose for you! Don't let trouble keep you from fulfilling His assignment. Don't run. Don't drop out of ministry. Don't quit reaching out.

Trouble doesn't disqualify you. In fact, trouble might better equip you! How? In times of trouble, you realize you can't rely on yourself, your strength, your ability, or your power.

The realization that your power isn't enough will bring you to a place of deeper dependence on God.

The realization that your power isn't enough will bring you to a place of deeper dependence on God. Respond to trouble with a radical dependence on Him!

Experiencing emotions isn't a lack of faith.

Early one morning after receiving the devastating diagnosis, I called Alton Garrison, our former pastor, my mentor, and friend. I poured out everything about Cindy, about cancer, and about the other situation I was dealing with that was so upsetting. Alton just listened. Before we hung up, he prayed a powerful prayer over me and Cindy. As he prayed, I put my head on my desk and wept. It was the first time I had allowed myself to feel the full weight of those emotions.

In that moment I learned an important truth: Experiencing emotions is not a lack of faith.

It's okay—in fact, it's healthy—to put a voice to what you feel. It's okay to cry. I needed that. I'm so thankful I had a safe place to have that conversation.

In times of uncertainty, take a faith-step in response to the fear.

A few days after we were plunged into this challenge I told Cindy, "We need to increase our giving." She immediately agreed, "Absolutely. Of course. This is a wonderful time to give more." We decided to increase our tithe by one hundred dollars a week for the duration of the journey. Why did we do that? That seems counterintuitive, but we wanted to fight the natural selfishness that comes with uncertainty, fear, and trouble.

> **In times of uncertainty, take a faith-step in response to the fear.**

Selfishness naturally happens when you're sick. It's not a sinful response; it's normal. When you're sick, sickness dominates your thinking. Your focus is on you:

Will I survive?
What must I do next?
How do I endure the pain?
What am I going to miss?

Your focus turns inward, and you hold on to what you have. It's almost a reflex. You find safety in certainty.

By increasing our giving, we sent three messages. First, each week we wrote the check we sent a powerful message to ourselves: Our trust is in the Lord. We refused to allow circumstances to dictate our focus. Instead of hanging on, we were letting go. Our hands were open. We wouldn't become selfish and inward focused, but would trust and give more!

Second, we sent a message to the Enemy. I don't know if Satan sees my tithe checks, but I hope he does! We wanted him to know: *Cancer isn't going to stop us from trusting in a faithful God. In fact, it will make us trust Him more. If you think cancer is going to knock us off-course, you better think again. The Lord is faithful!*

Third, we sent a message to the Lord: "We trust You. You are our Source, our Protector, and our Provider. Our trust is in You."

I'm not saying every person must give more money to God's work when they get sick, but that's the faith-step we took. It's a powerful principle: In times of uncertainty, take a faith-step in response to the fear.

- Fight the tendency to be selfish.
- Increase your giving.
- Do something for someone else.
- Share your faith.
- Stay engaged in your area of ministry.

Whatever you do, don't let trouble change trust!

God can and will use your trouble to minister to others.

God can use trouble to protect you and position you for His help and blessing. That perspective will change the way you view trouble. It would be awesome if you could see ahead of time how

God is going to use your trouble, but trusting in Him means making the decision, *I don't know how, or when or where, but I trust the Lord, that He is in this and will use it for my help and His glory.*

Immediately after sharing Cindy's diagnosis, we started hearing from people who were praying. We got cards, letters, texts and e-mails from over one hundred of our missionaries. Pastors and leaders across the country started texting me. Hundreds prayed and offered help.

I learned something from Cindy's decision to share this experience with others. Too many times people worry about being a burden to others, so they retreat into isolation and fight their battle alone. We've watched that so many times. It's easy to do, but not wise or biblical. We need each other. We're a family—a great, big, loving, praying family. Knowing that people were standing with us was an incredible encouragement and powerful support.

> **At the end of all the "what if" questions is Jesus!**

I challenge you, when difficulty comes, share your struggle and receive the support of God's people.

Sharing the journey was the right decision for us. It let the family of God be what God designed them to be. We read every Facebook post, every text, every e-mail, and every card.

"What if" thoughts are normal.

You might think, *Rod, you and Cindy have remarkable faith. I could never go through that without fear.* I didn't say we went through this experience without fear. We're human. On April 28, we went to the hospital for the surgery. As we sat and waited to be called, I wrote an update in my journal:

We're at the hospital, waiting to check in for the Cryoablation procedure. They're going to blast the tumor with super cold gas and freeze it. I'll admit, I've had quite a few "what if" thoughts.

I did. I went all the way with those thoughts. Cindy and I never really talked about it, but I know she did too because the night before the surgery, she showed me where everything important and valuable was in our house. She had never done that before. She didn't say why she was showing me, but I understood. She was also having "what if" thoughts.

I think those thoughts are normal. I also don't think those thoughts indicate a lack of faith. Our "what if" thoughts, in fact, are the entire reason why we need faith. Remember what Shadrach, Meshach, and Abednego said to King Nebuchadnezzar? Essentially, they said, "Even if God doesn't save us, we won't bow down to the statue you set up."

Job said: "Though he slay me, yet will I hope in him" (Job 13:15).

What were these men doing? They were asking and answering the "what if" question. We honor them as heroes of faith, but they recognized the reality of their situations.

What are we doing when we ask the "what if" questions? We're being honest with God and defining the problem. Faith isn't found in the question, but in the answer to the question. Our answer was: "If we get the best report, we trust God. If we get a difficult report, we still trust God."

At the end of all the "what if" questions is Jesus! We feel peace in the presence of Jesus. We are in His hands—which is absolutely the best place to be!

The Rest of the Story

On Wednesday, April 5, Cindy shared her diagnosis with the Wednesday night ladies group. They prayed for her. The choir prayed for her. Our open journey had begun.

The next morning, I posted this:

Last Friday Cindy was diagnosed with cancer in her kidney. Although we haven't said anything on Facebook, we didn't keep it a secret. Cindy strongly feels she should walk this journey openly with our church family, knowing that many others face similar journeys.

It's been a bit of a whirlwind. We haven't even had the chance to share what's going on with all our prayer partners and friends.

This morning, we had an appointment with the surgeon. . . . They caught the cancer at an unusually small size. As a result, they're going to be able to do a procedure called Cryoablation. Essentially, they biopsy the tumor and freeze it at the same time. They destroy the tumor by freezing it to below 100° Celsius.

The procedure is minimally invasive with only a one-night hospital stay and recovery of about a week. They expect no radiation or chemotherapy. It's our hope to schedule the procedure as soon as possible within the next couple of weeks.

Then, I shared what for us is the most powerful part of the story, which is that the story actually *began* two and a half years earlier, even though we couldn't have realized it at the time. The week of Thanksgiving 2014, Cindy experienced unexplained renal failure. A nurse called me from the doctor's office and said, "We're sending Cindy to the hospital. In fact, the doctor told me to follow her to make sure she gets there. We expect her to be put in ICU."

Cindy's numbers were extremely frightening. It was a tense, challenging time for us. The doctors weren't sure what would happen.

Cindy spent the rest of that week and Thanksgiving weekend in the hospital. They checked her blood levels every two hours for the next four or five days. We spent a lot of time in prayer. Even after she was discharged, the trial wasn't over. For three months, Cindy had to live with a catheter and continued appointments with the doctor. We cancelled trips and plans and a much-needed week of rest. We had no choice.

At the time, it was incredibly difficult to understand this turn of events. We asked why but there was no answer from God. Heaven was silent. It didn't make sense; it didn't seem fair. We just struggled and wondered and trusted.

During that time, a doctor in our church, Pat Knott, connected us with a wonderful urologist, Dr. Gayle Jones. Gayle is a committed Christian who loves God. She took over Cindy's care.

After Cindy finally got better, we discovered Dr. Jones was also ultracautious. She scheduled regular tests to monitor Cindy's health and make sure everything was okay. Even more than two years later, Dr. Jones still ran tests and examined Cindy every six weeks or so. During one of those routine tests, Dr. Jones discovered the tumor. Without those scans, it's likely the tumor would have gone unnoticed for months, maybe longer. Instead, the doctor discovered it early, while it was still very small.

Now, looking in the "rearview mirror," we understood what we couldn't understand two and a half years earlier. God, who knows all things, put us exactly where we needed to be. He put us with the right doctor at the right time. God spoke to that doctor and directed her to continue a high standard of care and watchfulness. If the renal failure had never happened, we never would have been with Dr. Jones and the tumor could have grown unchecked. All things had worked together for our good.

How many times have you faced trouble or hardship and wondered: *Where is God in this? How could a loving God allow this? How could God let this happen to me?* One day, what doesn't make sense now will make perfect sense. And you'll discover that, all along, God was working and moving and orchestrating things you couldn't see.

You might be asking, "Rod, are you saying you believe God caused Cindy's renal failure?" I'm not saying that. It might have been an attack from Satan. It sure felt like it then. Like any number of awful situations, it might have been a natural result of living in this sin-filled world. Regardless of what it was or where it came from, God used it for His perfect purposes! He does all things well!

Cindy had the surgery on Friday. The procedure took an hour. When the doctor came out to give me the report he said, "We got it. The procedure went perfectly. We killed the tumor." I almost started crying! We went home that afternoon. Cindy didn't even need to stay in the hospital but could recover at home, which made her superhappy.

The doctor suggested she stay in bed and rest for several days. Sunday morning, during the 10 o'clock service, I sensed some movement behind me . . . someone sitting in Cindy's usual seat. I turned around to see who it was—and saw Cindy! Though tired and hurting, she just wanted to be in God's house.

That morning Pastor Brad led us in the hymn, "Blessed Assurance." Cindy was too sore to stand, but she was sitting right behind me. My eyes filled with tears as I heard her singing loudly:

Perfect submission, all is at rest
I in my Savior am happy and blessed
Watching and waiting, looking above,
Filled with His goodness, lost in His love.
This is my story, this is my song,
Praising my Savior, all the day long.

The Lord is faithful! We've walked through the cancer journey with others. We know it can be up and down. We know it's often a roller coaster. We get that. Cindy will have a scan every three months to see if the cancer has returned. The first two have come back all clear. But regardless of the results of future scans, we've already determined our response. If the cancer never returns, the Lord is faithful. If cancer rears its ugly head again, the Lord is faithful. He has demonstrated His love and care to us. We trust Him. He is faithful.

I don't know what you are facing right now or what you might face in the future. The leadership journey has its ups and downs, but through it all the Lord is with you. You may feel alone and forgotten, but you're not. Your Heavenly Father is watching over you. He's caring for you and protecting you. He knows exactly where you are, what you're going through, what you feel, and what you need. Never forget: *The Lord is faithful!*

A final note

If you're in the middle of a difficult journey, I would be honored to pray with you. Feel free to e-mail me directly:

rloy@firstnlr.com

About the Author

Rod Loy has been in full-time pastoral ministry for over thirty-five years. He serves as senior pastor at FirstNLR, in North Little Rock, Arkansas, a multi-site church with thirteen campuses and an online attendance of more than 40,000 weekly (www.firstnlr.tv). FirstNLR gives over a million dollars to missions every year and has helped to plant more than 1,200 churches in sixty-three nations. His passion for missions has taken him to over fifty different countries.

Rod is also the Vice President of Strategic Initiatives for Project Rescue, a ministry that rescues women and children from human trafficking. Project Rescue operates over a dozen rescue homes on multiple continents.

He is the author of *3 Questions, Immediate Obedience,* and *After the Honeymoon.* Rod's unique approach to leadership has led him to adventures in the real world, including working as a volunteer lifeguard at a water park. A former children's pastor, Rod has helped develop the Faith Case® curriculum for children and is still actively involved with kids. In fact, his office is in the preschool department!

He and his wife, Cindy, have been married for over thirty years and have two sons: Tyler and his wife, Emilie, and Parker and his wife, Meredith. They have two grandchildren Evie Brooke and Maverick. The Loys live in North Little Rock, Arkansas.

For more resources from Rod Loy visit www.rodloy.com or email him at rloy@firstnlr.com.

Other books available from Rod Loy